COMMERCIAL ACTING IN L.A.

A SESSION DIRECTOR'S GUIDE

> "If you don't know the information covered in this book, I guarantee you are losing work."

BY SHAAN SHARMA

ILLUSTRATIONS BY PAUL LOUDON

WARNING! ADULT CONTENT AND LANGUAGE!—DISCLAIMER:
Do not read this if you like to make a big deal out of nothing, have a weak stomach, are easily offended, or not yet allowed to see R-rated movies. The following contains naughty but fun language. Read at your own risk. Side effects include meaningless euphoria, loose stools, pregnancy, and cancer of the ass-bone. (Wait. Maybe I'm not supposed to put adult content in the disclaimer…) In other words, I am not responsible for any negative reactions you have to this book and am entirely responsible for any and all positive reactions you have to this book.

YOU. HAVE. BEEN. WARNED.

DEDICATED TO:

The Actors, who get up every day and work hard to achieve success, oftentimes in survival jobs that are neither their passion nor an accurate reflection of their potential, in spite of the odds against them.

The Actors, who are not only willing but dying to sacrifice their heart, soul, and body on the world stage to help tell you a story, one that could transport you, thrill you, or move you to tears, to joy, to laughter, or to action.

The Actors, who have dedicated themselves to the study of what it means to be human and all the many types of human experiences and relationships, as dark and bright as they may be.

And so, to the Actors, I just want to say thank you and encourage you to remember:

You can't fail if you never quit.

Copyright © 2014 by Shaan Sharma.

All Rights Reserved. No part of this publication may be reproduced, digitally stored, or transmitted in any form or by any means, electronic, mechanical, photocopying, recording or otherwise, without the prior written permission of the copyright holders. For permission, contact:

shaan@shaansharma.com

ISBN: 978-0-9904080-0-0

CONTENTS

INTRODUCTION   1
Who am I that you should listen to me?

CHAPTER ONE   10
A tale of two cities:
The difference between commercial and theatrical casting.

CHAPTER TWO   19
Get out before you ever get in.
Are you cray-cray?
Why do you even want to do this??

CHAPTER THREE   24
Who am I? What have I become?!
Take stock of your look.
Design a better one. Stick to it.

CHAPTER FOUR   27
Learn how to ACT, dummy.
Get improv and acting training.

CHAPTER FIVE   53
Pix or you don't exist.
Headshots, Glorious Headshots.

CHAPTER SIX   59
We don't take headshots.
Online casting services you need to use.

CHAPTER SEVEN   68
No auditions for you! Why you need an agent and how to get one.
Also, managers.

CHAPTER EIGHT   76
Get your sh*t straight, son.
What you need to begin your journey.

CHAPTER NINE   88
OMG!! An audition!
What to do when you get the call/text/email that you have
an audition.

CHAPTER TEN   121
Shoulder to shoulder:
How to fool us into thinking you actually
know what you're doing at an audition.

CHAPTER ELEVEN   149
F*ck! I should have said or done this! Argghh!
What to do and not do after the audition.

CHAPTER TWELVE   152
The (Occasional) Epitome of Awkward: The Callback.

CHAPTER THIRTEEN   164
The Tease: Avail!
So close . . . and yet so far away.

CHAPTER FOURTEEN   167
The Orgasm: Booking. YOU booked it?
You booked it!
Holy shit! You're for realz now!

CHAPTER FIFTEEN   170
The Money Shot: The shoot and life on a commercial set. MAKE IT RAIN.

CHAPTER SIXTEEN   175
Free Money! Residuals, re-negotiations, holding fees, and other things you can't control but may pay you tons of money you didn't expect.

CHAPTER SEVENTEEN   181
What now?
The boring day-to-day life of an actor and how to kill time between jobs.

CHAPTER EIGHTEEN   186
Peon Love: How to get called in to more commercial casting offices.
(SPOILER: If you want to be interesting, be interested and don't be a dickhead.)

BONUS CHAPTER NINETEEN   194
Daddy needs a new Maserati: How to get your kids into commercial acting so you can live your unfulfilled dreams vicariously through them and steal all their money to live like a baller before they're old enough to know what's going on and emancipate themselves from you AND how to not act like an obnoxious stage parent.

SAMPLE RESUME   202

SOCIAL MEDIA LINKS   203

INTRODUCTION
Who am I that you should listen to me?

I'm a session director for many of Los Angeles's top commercial casting directors (CD's). If you've auditioned for commercials in LA over the past seven years, chances are you've met or seen me already. I am the only Indian session director in town, so I'd like to think that's memorable. If you have not yet had the pleasure of meeting me, well how sad for you. I work all the time all over LA, so somebody reading this is not getting out as much they should . . . not gonna point fingers or name names.

So what is a session director and how is that different from a casting director, you may ask. Short answer: We run your commercial auditions.

Good commercial casting directors consistently bring their clients great talent options for their projects' needs. They know LA's talent pool inside and out, have the resources and network to find great options for even the most random roles—like conjoined twin biathletes—and possess the business know-how to deftly navigate the minefield of being in the middle of corporate clients, producers, directors, actors, agents, and managers, all of whom have their own needs and agendas. They're also small business owners with employees and offices to manage.

A CD's whole day can easily be consumed with crafting and releasing effective casting notices (breakdowns) for jobs, poring over thousands of actor photos that were submitted for roles and deciding who to call in for an audition, helping address the needs of the clients, and negotiating with agents over rates or other details, or being pitched by agents wanting to bring in their actors. Production timelines have become so short thanks to technology that clients now routinely expect casting directors to cast a whole project in just a couple of days, when years ago they would have been given a week. On top of all that, thanks to stiff competition from other CD's, or shrinking budgets, clients often expect more work for less pay. When CD's are not digging out of an avalanche of work, they're trying to generate new work to be consumed by. Doesn't that all sound so fun and glamorous? So forgive their eccentricities. They have to deal with a LOT of shit.

Because of all that, casting directors don't always have the time to personally run their casting sessions and work with the actors to get the performances they need, or the technical expertise to run the equipment and software used to capture the auditions and present them. That's where we come in.

They hire us, session directors, to handle the whole day of casting. We're usually the only ones you interact with when you come in the room. We're the ones who tell you what's going on and what to do, direct you, and fix you when your only-high-school-drama-class acting training is letting you down. We put you on "tape," an anachronism: No one uses tape anymore, but we still call it that for lack of an updated replacement word. We say good or bad things about you, your attitude, or your performance to the casting directors and clients, so if you suck really bad or you mistreat us or our comrades, chances are you won't be invited back.

In short, you usually don't deal with the CD at commercial auditions. You deal with me and others like me. I think it's fair to say that your relationship with session directors is as important as your relationship with casting directors, just for a different reason. Most of us float around and work for many CD's all over town. Today, I might be running Home Depot auditions for Michael Sanford at Exclusive. Tomorrow, I could be running the Verizon callback for Gabrielle Schary at Sessions West on the Westside. You never know. We never know. But you will see many of us all over town.

Here's how it breaks down: casting directors drum up or competitively bid on casting jobs from their director, production, or corporate friends/contacts, and deal with all the back-office work, but to you, the actor, all you care about is that they have the power to decide who to call in for an audition. That factor alone puts them at the top of your priority list because you can't get work and get rich and famous without first getting the audition that gives you the chance to book the job. But what ultimately gets you the job is your performance, and session directors are the ones responsible for getting that from you, capturing it, and presenting it. After years of experience, we know how to get great performances out of actors in seconds, making it possible to audition an actor every two and a half minutes for a seven-hour casting session.

Thanks to this arrangement, CD's can focus on everything else they need to do while we hold down the casting fort for them. Before the day's session begins, we work together to set the action and blocking that the director, ad agency, producer and/or corporate clients need to see for each role, and then the CD's are free to go handle the business end while we rock out the auditions.

In the office, casting directors are assisted by casting associates (senior level) or assistants (junior level).

They help with the back-office work, including communicating with the directors, clients, ad agencies, production and agents, and talent scouting. They might also help with prep: the writing and releasing of casting breakdowns and the calling in and scheduling of talent for auditions.

Casting and session directors are also sometimes assisted by lobby assistants, the brave men and women that make our life easier by greeting you actors as you enter, checking you in, making sure you get the copy and other important details, put you in groups, and whatever else is necessary so that as soon as our studio door opens, the next group is ready to come in and nail it. And they usually write up the cue cards, known as "boards," the big pieces of paper hanging in the studio with your lines on it. (Lobby assistants are often girls, and girls usually have better handwriting than boys, and most session directors are boys, so it falls to lobby assistants to write the boards so that you can actually read them.) The best lobby assistants help us be efficient so that we're not wasting time and our room can stay busy auditioning actors (also so we can have our full lunch break; oh my god I'm so hungry by 1pm).

The way you should see it is that casting directors call you in to work with us. If you're smart, you'll start making an effort to get to know us. Sure, sometimes, if we have a lot of cancellations or if our relationship with a casting director is very strong, we may be able to call in a friend or two to audition for a job we're running, as long as they are a good fit and with office approval. More important, though, is the fact that we have the greatest impact on how well your audition is going to go, so wouldn't you rather that experience start with a warm greeting of mutual recognition and admiration?

Session directors are actually doing two jobs. Most actors currently call us "camera guys." That's sexist and mildly insulting. First, there are some great women running sessions, and second, we do a lot more than jockey a camera. Now, indeed, some casting directors choose to direct their own casting sessions and don't need a session director. They just need someone to run the camera and equipment, so they, or the studio, will hire a camera operator, or Cam Op, or what most actors have hitherto called a (cringe) camera "guy."

You see, a casting director rents a studio at a casting facility to conduct a casting session. The studio is responsible for providing them with a camera operator as part of the rental fee. So, the studio pays us to do that part of the job. If the casting director isn't going to direct the session, then they need to hire a session director, and they usually just pay the camera operator to do that job too. So, we get paid twice for two different jobs: running the equipment for the studio, and directing the session for the casting director. Pretty sweet, huh?

I prefer to do both. I almost never just Cam Op any more. With seven years of session directing and camera operating under my belt, I am a machine. It slows me down to have someone else in the mix. Plus, as an actor myself (most SD's are), I have so much fun directing sessions. I get to play with other actors all day every day and help them book work.

If, after reading this, you never look at session directors the same way again, I'll have done my job. We're on your side. We're there to help you give a performance that will get you booked. Trust us. Listen to us.

With that said, what follows is a step-by-step guide on how to make sure that the reason you're not booking commercials isn't because you don't know basic shit and not doing everything right that is within your scope of control. Sure, the information in this book is going to be immensely valuable for a newbie, but even experienced actors will find useful tips and advice. If you read this studiously, you will be more effective and you will probably book more (or a lot more) work, but obviously, there's no guarantee. You're getting an insider's view from someone who has worked on both sides of the camera for the top CD's who work for the top directors, ad agencies, producers, and companies in the world.

I should also mention that this book makes no pretense of being politically correct, and in case you're too dense to figure it out as you read it, this is written with tons of sarcasm, and I poke fun at us as actors and many aspects of our business because it's entertaining and FUNNY . . . to ME. Nor is this book 100% accurate when it comes to laws, rules, facts, and figures, though I did try my best. I think I need to cover my ass and say something like: none of what follows should be taken as legal, medical, or financial advice and that you should always consult with your doctor before beginning any intense fitness program. If, at any time, you experience a prolonged numbness or tingling sensation, put down the Shake Weight. You've had enough.

The point is, I absolutely LOVE our craft, our business, and the wonderful people in it, in every role. It's just that the only way I could make myself write this was to have as much fun doing so without any care or concern for perfection or the delicate, dainty feelings of those who read it, who are overwhelmingly going to be sensitive actors. At times it may feel like I'm being critical of us actors, directors, ad agency peeps or corporate clients, but just remember to put it in the proper perspective. I wouldn't be doing right by you if I sugar-coated anything, because casting and the challenges we face as actors are serious business. We're insane for wanting to do this. Most actors I meet are brilliant, gorgeous, high-potential people who could be changing the world with their energy and talent but have instead chosen to pursue a career in a tough business that may never love them back. I NEED to tell it to you straight up. No bullshit. Besides, deep down we both know you like the rough stuff, don't ya, you perv? If you've read *Fifty Shades of Grey*, nod.

I was born and raised in Minnesnowta, USA where it's FREEZING nine months out of the year. I was the only Indian kid in an all-white high school, skinny, lanky, devoid of social and fashion sensibilities with big ugly glasses, a bad student and an emotionally volatile artist on top of that. I barely survived and it's a miracle I didn't end up on *COPS*, *Hoarders* or *Intervention*, so give me a frikkin' break, man. I mock and love everyone and everything equally. Except spiders and mosquitoes. That, my friends, is ALL hate.

But I digress. Shall we dive in?

CHAPTER ONE
A tale of two cities:
The difference between commercial and theatrical casting.

Okay. The simplest way to describe the difference between the commercial and theatrical sides of the business is that they have virtually nothing in common except that they both employ actors. It's a little less cut and dried than that, but that comes pretty close.

Here's why: They serve two entirely separate masters/purposes.

The commercial world serves corporate America. When you audition for a commercial project, whether it's a commercial, industrial, or print job, it's all for the purpose of marketing a product or service, or creating corporate media assets or training materials and the like. Some companies prefer to do everything themselves; "in-house." Others farm out part or all of that work to advertising agencies, production companies, directors and casting directors. In any case, the company has the final say on everything. It's their money, their brand, their project. They are the "client." However, we in casting often refer to everyone who works on the client side (excluding us) as "clients," because the directors, producers and ad agencies are *our* clients, while the company we're all working for is *the* client.

The client or their ad agency comes up with the marketing plan, which might include audio/video content. The ad agency pitches its audio/video concepts to the client for approval. Once approved, the ad agency will hire a production company to produce the project and a director to direct the project. The director or producer then hires the casting director for any acting talent needs. That's when a CD will put out a breakdown and hold first-call audition sessions. When those are complete, the ad agency and director choose their favorite actors to either present to the client for approval or, more frequently, invite to a callback (a second-round audition), usually with the director, producers, ad agency and sometimes even the client present in the room. After the callback, the director and ad agency make their final picks, and present them to the client for approval. That's how you end up getting cast in a commercial. The important part to realize is that your audition is seen and evaluated not only by the director, ad agents, and producers, who are all creative or artistic people like ourselves, but by corporate client reps, like Pepsi's marketing VP or whatever, who may not know much about our craft at all, and it's their final decision.

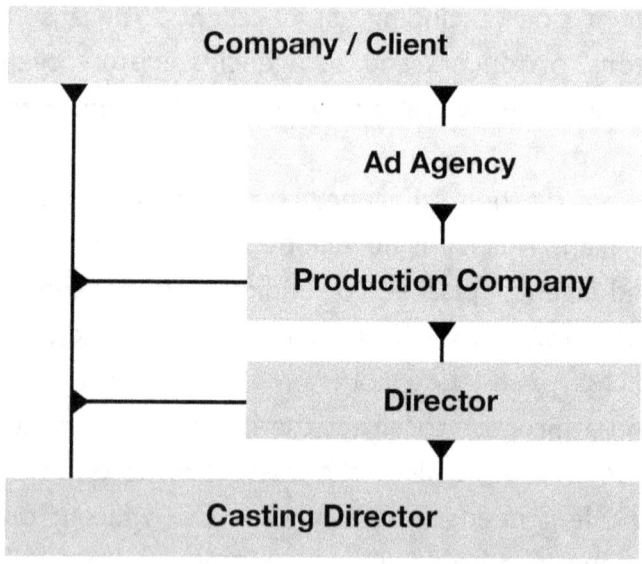

So, when you come in to audition for a commercial, we tell you exactly what we need you to do because the director, ad agency and/or client has already told us exactly what they want to see you do. Walk over here, look up, say this line as if you're excited, and then hug your husband. We don't have time for you to write a ten-page backstory for your character or work out your objective, wants and obstacles. I'll give you your damn backstory and objective: You're you, you're hungry and you want Brand X potato chips. Walk over there, eat one, and look like you like it. Simple. Done. NEXT!

The theatrical side, meaning TV, film, and theater, is more about the actor's role and our craft. It's where our art form can exist in all its creative glory. It's where you truly are the professional artist, where your skills and training will clearly set you apart from the others. It's where you get to be more involved in the creative process of storytelling. It's what we all love about acting, making choices and having an experience.

In a theatrical audition, we would never dream of telling you what to do. When you go into a theatrical audition, the casting director may ask you if you have any questions or clear up any common traps or misinterpretations of the material, but beyond that, they want to see what *you* would do. The theatrical side of the business exists to serve fellow artists: the directors, producers, and writers, not a corporation and its products or services that usually have nothing to do with the arts. They, on the theatrical side, want and need our creativity, our interpretation, our mastery over bringing out the human experience in imaginary circumstances, and from a casting perspective, they're looking for a variety of choices, great performances, and types. They celebrate the differences in our work.

You might ask, "Why aren't commercial auditions like that? Why do commercial casting sessions need direction in the first place? Why can't they be like theatrical auditions where you come in and do your thing, your interpretation of the copy, and then leave it at that?" Well, because of the extremely particular needs of the corporate marketing machine, left alone you will almost never do it "right," a concept that doesn't really exist in the craft of acting generally but very much does in commercial projects. The clients want to make sure you do exactly what they have in their minds and on their storyboards. If they could control every movement of your body, every sound of your voice, the intonation of every word you speak of their perfectly (in their minds) crafted commercial copy, they would gladly do it. If we could all be perfect little puppets to fit perfectly into their ad campaigns, all with perfect hands, teeth and skin, "aspirational" (read: hot but not too hot) looks, and logo and pattern-free wardrobe, it would be marketing nirvana for them. Alas, they are left having to deal with real human beings (yuck!), free will, and a variety of shapes, sizes, and dentistry. So, they need us in casting to try to make you all uniformly "great." Trust me, commercial actors will rue the day computer generated people become indistinguishable from real, human actors.

Also, let's be honest, left to your own devices, you actors will almost always do too much or do wacky shit, trying to wow us with your "ability" and "talent" in every audition. Usually, more than anything else, we need to tone you down and remind you that, dude, you're just sitting there eating soup. It doesn't need to be a whole production. And would it kill you to smile like a normal person instead of looking like Martin Short in *Clifford*? We know you're "acting," but surely, you've discovered along the way that the best acting is when we can't tell that you are, in fact, acting. And, truth be told, some of you have been trained wrong by some of the weird commercial workshops or acting classes out there. It's not your fault. You didn't know better, but we can tell. Relax. It's going to be okay. You're here now. You're safe.

The differences between the two worlds also explain why we need a more professional casting studio setup with lights, pro-cameras, mics, props, and computers and software for commercial casting sessions, as opposed to just a simple camcorder in a trailer or office at theatrical castings. Corporate America demands that our media—photos/video/audio of your auditions—be of the best quality and leave as little to the imagination as possible. Why? Because a lot of decision makers who aren't in the entertainment business are going to be looking at our casting sessions. We want to make it easy for them to see and hear everything clearly and envision the final product. It puts them at ease. Our casting media is itself a product the production has paid for to present talent options to their client, so it has to look and sound good. Casting facilities compete with each other to offer better amenities for visiting clients, more polished presentations, and higher-tech solutions.

It tends to be easier to get represented commercially by agents and managers, simply because commercial casting directors usually need to present many more options to their clients than theatrical CD's do. For example, a theatrical CD might only audition 15 or 20 people for a co-star role that needs filling. Based on his or her experience and knowledge of the talent pool, that's probably all that's needed to find someone great. There isn't a corporate client breathing down his or her neck expecting to see 100 people per role, if for no other reason than to feel like they got their money's worth.

Also, because corporate clients know exactly what type they want, they don't need *you* as much. They just want to see a ton of choices. They're not looking for a performance, sometimes, but a look. The suburban mom. The schlubby sports fan. The aristocratic white-collar professional. The hipster. Which is why crafting a good commercial look for yourself and dressing appropriately for the role at each audition is an essential part of booking commercial work. They, the ad agents or marketing people, are trying to find the actors with the faces and the looks that match the storyboards which they sold to and were approved by their client. We are constantly amazed at who the commercial clients end up booking for certain roles because it's not always the best actor, in our eyes anyway. I don't want to make it sound like you don't even need to know how to act to book commercials, but the fact of the matter is a lot of bad actors are booking commercial work every day, while few bad actors are booking roles on the top TV shows and films.

Another way to look at it is this: They don't have time for you to gain or lose 50 pounds, grow hair, or otherwise transform yourself for a role. Yes, we all know that you can play anything because you're SO talented, but clients often need to book someone who already looks and feels the part. The commercial production timeline is too fast, and the eventual commercial spot will only be 15 or 30 seconds, so there's not a lot of time to establish characters. It's like a mini movie in which the actors have to visually communicate their role in the story immediately, often non-verbally. That's why it often comes down to a look for commercial work and why you need to be very thoughtful and intentional about your looks and what kinds of roles you're trying to book.

It is true, however, that you won't have a prayer of booking *some* campaigns unless you've got some serious acting chops. If you've got the combination of a good commercial or unique look and good training, you will book a commercial eventually. At that point, it's a numbers game.

CHAPTER TWO
Get out before you ever get in.
Are you cray-cray?
Why do you even want to do this??

So, why do actors do commercials? Well, the *money*, of course. If you book a national commercial, you can make tens of thousands of dollars, even hundreds of thousands of dollars. All from *one* job. If you book a co-star role on a network TV show, you might make a thousand bucks, probably much less after taxes and commissions. If you booked a guest star (you go!) on a network show, you might make a few thousand dollars. You have to be a series regular on a network show or a lead in a union feature film to make the kind of money you can make from one national TV commercial.

If you book a national TV commercial, you could make enough money to quit your serving job, get a physical trainer, a dialect coach, buy better food and clothing, join the best acting studio, improv group, and all the other things we need to be doing to compete here in LA in the Super Bowl of acting. We're competing with the best actors in the world, some of whom have financial resources or support that the rest of us don't have, but the industry doesn't care about what's fair. They just need good actors, and if you're good, you'll work. Period. So if you work hard, you will become good, maybe even great, and you will book work. That's actually very fair. Commercials can subsidize your TV/film career until it takes off, but even then, even A-list celebs do commercials. It just pays too well to not do them.

Just as important, commercial work can be incredibly visible and create potentially life- or career-changing opportunities. If you end up booking a spokesperson job for a major company, it's like winning the lottery. Stephanie Courtney has made millions from her role as "Flo" for Progressive Auto Insurance. Same with Carly Foulkes, the T-Mobile girl and Paul Marcarelli, the "Verizon Guy". Beck Bennett's AT&T commercials gave him the visibility that ultimately landed him a place in the cast of *Saturday Night Live*.

But beyond the possible riches and fame, commercials really impact our popular culture and national discussion. Great ads can make us want to cry, laugh, tell our loved ones we love them, or change the world. It feels amazing to be a part of a great campaign that doesn't just peddle some crap, but is actually really funny, innovative, effects social change or inspires people. Great ad slogans become part of our vernacular. Who can forget Nike's "Just do it" or Budweiser's "Wazzup" or Life Alert's "I've fallen and I can't get up!" With great advertising, even something as unglamorous as the California Milk Processor Board can infiltrate our everyday life with their slogan "Got Milk?"

From the brilliant minds of commercial clients, writers, directors and advertising professionals come some of the most entertaining and impactful short forms of visual storytelling. So much so that we actually *look forward* to seeing the commercials during the Super Bowl. How counterintuitive is that? Commercials are usually a pain in our ass as consumers because we're inundated with them. They're everywhere. We can't escape them.

But if they're done well, we actually want to see them and will even share them with our friends and families, which could mean sharing your face too, if you're in one of them.

There are many great reasons to do commercials. Some actors believe they are above commercial work, and good for them if they are. I'm not. I actually love it. I love the business of casting them and acting in them. I also love them for the opportunity they are for great personal reward. Income from my FedEx commercial saved my little heinie more than once when I was struggling financially. Besides, when else, other than being in a studio feature film, would I have had the opportunity to have a computer-generated version of me made and broadcast across the country?!

Now, are *you* ready to "sell out" and "reduce yourself to a human prop" in a national commercial about, say, selling fried chicken? Yes? Sweet. Welcome to the club.

Be prepared to audition a lot. That means driving all over town, waiting in waiting rooms, changing clothes like an outfit-conscious sufferer of multiple personality disorder, and enduring the feelings of being one small guppy in a seemingly infinite and replenishing ocean of talent. It's a war of attrition, really. If you stick with it long enough, you'll start figuring it all out while others with less endurance drop out. Then you'll be left in a pool of veterans who just paid off their house with their last two commercials. "Did you see my new car? I call it the Comcast Lexus!"

Committing to pursuing commercial work is step number one. Make sure you're mentally prepared for it and adjust your expectations appropriately. You might audition 100 times a year and book just four or five jobs but still clear six figures as a result. Just put your head down and charge forth. For most of us, it's a ton of fun, always something new, we get to see friends every day and play pretend for a living, and it beats being stuck in a cubicle doing data entry or some other shitness.

Also, just know that there is plenty of work out there for serious, committed, and good actors. You can do it if you work hard and keep learning. There is a *ton* of commercial work. There are tens of thousands of commercial projects made every year. Every business needs to market itself, and those campaigns need talent. You are a product for which there is a demand, so let's take a look at how to do the most with what you've got.

CHAPTER THREE
Who am I? What have I become?!
Take stock of your look.
Design a better one. Stick to it.

Watch commercials and you'll get a good sense of what types of looks book. Look at yourself in the mirror and really ask yourself, "Who am I?" Are you a man or woman? Old or young? Hot or not? Quirky or normal?

Fit or fat? Stylish or plain? Professional or working class? Would a mustache help or hurt you—and I mean the men also? How about a beard? Should you ditch or keep the glasses? Is your hair hip or out of a 90's salon look-book? You need to take stock and get clear about what kinds of looks you can pull off and what kinds of roles you'd be a good fit for. There's no point in getting pictures taken if you're just going to change everything after, so do this part first.

If you're not really self-aware, it might be helpful to ask your friends and family or Facebook "friends" what types of roles they think you could play. You might just learn a little more about yourself and how others perceive you, a nice little bonus. You're welcome. And I'm sorry.

And don't lie to yourself. For Pete's sake, if you're six feet tall and weigh 100 pounds, you're just not going to get booked as "Overweight Man on the Treadmill." Just don't even try. Just accept it. It's not going to happen for you. I'm sorry. You're emaciated. Own it.

Also, if you're in your 30's, and you think you look like your late teens or early 20's, you don't. Just shut your mouth. You *don't*. Besides, someone who actually is 18 will look more 18 than you will. Deal with it. You're OLD.

Overall, there aren't really that many main types of roles. We tend to fall into obvious and general categories like the college student, a young mom or dad, the young business professional, an athlete, the blue-collar worker, the executive, etc. As far as look categories go, you'll fall into one of three general buckets: model types (Hottie McHottersons), aspirational types (generally attractive), and character types (only your mom tells you you're handsome).

If there are any changes you want to make to your look, set some goals. As an actor, you yourself are the product you are trying to sell, so design and package it well. From fitness to hygiene to style, put some thought into your look while being true to who you are and being the best you.

CHAPTER FOUR
Learn how to ACT, dummy.
Get improv and acting training.

So, I just finished explaining that you don't *need* to know how to act to book commercials, but if you want to seriously increase your chances, you do. And honestly, before you go and get headshots and representation and dilute the pool of talent in this town, I kind of DEMAND that you learn how to act first, for your own sake. You wouldn't want to waste opportunities and burn bridges by being unprepared for them. It's a smaller town than you think, and you only get to make a first impression once, so hold your horses there, cowpoke. There is a huge amount of work that goes into being a good actor. Only amateurs think that actors just memorize their lines, and that if they're talented, great performances will just come out. That couldn't be further from the truth. More than any other factor, it takes good training, skill, consistent practice, and a strong work ethic.

While it is true that some people are naturally gifted actors and take more easily to being present in the moment, listening, responding, and behaving truthfully on-stage or on-camera, compare it to a naturally gifted athlete. They may be strong or fast, but they still need to learn the rules of the game, the plays and the strategies, train specific muscles or movements, and practice on a regular basis in order to compete at the highest level. In the acting business, there are also different games that require different applications of the acting craft and approaches to the work: drama, comedy, dramedy, procedural, single-camera, multi- camera, feature, short-form, one hour, and half hour, not to mention the tones of different shows within a genre or the styles and expectations of specific writers. All these games and requisite skills show up in commercial work, because there are commercials shot in almost all of these styles. Then, on top of that, there are jobs specific to the commercial world.

So don't fool yourself. Don't give people a reason to roll their eyes when you tell them you're an actor. Don't rush. Don't be a poser. You wouldn't call yourself an airplane pilot if you didn't know how to fly a plane. The same goes for acting. And I'm so sorry to tell you this, but no diploma or degree or acting class credit on your resume will prove to us that you're a good actor. The only thing that matters is the quality of the work you do in an audition. Roll up your sleeves and get to work. The good news is that the study of acting in the right environment can be a lot of fun, so much so that some actors become class junkies and never actually get in the actual game, which is fine if acting isn't how you want to make your living and is just a creative outlet or hobby. However, if you're reading this book, I'm assuming that you want to earn enough money as an actor to have a collection of vintage Bentleys on display in the garage of your 10,000 sq. ft. home in Malibu within the next 10 years . . . or whatever success means to you.

First things first. If you're brand spankin' new to acting, you might find that saying other people's words out loud and memorization are challenging. Get yourself into a good acting class that will help you develop these skills. If you want to practice on your own, just start reading books or magazines out loud. Try memorizing a small paragraph, and work your way up to a whole page. You wouldn't believe how many "actors" cannot handle copy; the words, and the dialogue. Casting directors will literally put the requirement in the breakdown, "must be good with dialogue," because way too many actors can't handle saying words.

It's weird; a lot of actors bum out when they get an audition for a role that has only a line or two, as if they are above it, and then freak out and can't handle it when they get one with five pages of dialogue. It stems from the fact that many wannabe actors lack training or are lazy. There's no way to hide the fact that you aren't a skilled actor or don't have a strong work ethic when you have lots of dialogue, so those not competent and therefore not confident, freak out. Casting directors try their best to weed those wannabes out.

Let me state it again for emphasis: learning and mastering a skill makes you competent, which makes you confident, which is when you're ready for prime time. Most people who move to LA to act don't know any better or are over-confident so they jump right into the game before they're ready to play and compete. Get your head on straight and build your foundation before you throw yourself into the fray where you'll be up against the people you see on TV and film every day.

The most important thing commercial agents look for on your resume is improv training. Improvisation is when you just make shit up on the spot. You can just roll with any given acting scenario. That's what's necessary in commercial auditions. Why? Because you're almost never given the script ahead of time since, technically, we're not allowed to ask you to prepare the material before you come audition. We need you to be able to listen, take direction, and think on your feet to put a great performance together quickly while also putting your own stank on it at the same time. You are a unique snowflake. No one else on earth is just like you, and improv training will help you loosen up, live in the moment, listen, find your voice, and create fearlessly in any acting situation. Improv teaches you to trust yourself and to recognize that your point of view is unique and entertaining. All of that is extremely helpful in commercial work.

But not all commercial work is supposed to be funny or entertaining. Sometimes, it calls for serious acting chops, in which case there is no substitute for real acting training. Get yourself into a good acting class or studio. Check out a bunch through what is known as an "audit." Most studios offer audits to prospective students as an opportunity to sit in on a class for free or for a small fee to get a sense of it and determine if it is a good fit for both parties. Audit as many as you can, and take your time in making a decision on which one to join. It's a *huge* decision. **Where you study will have the biggest impact on your career's trajectory.** I also highly recommend taking a class where you get to see yourself on camera. If you want to work on-camera, shouldn't you know and study how you look on-camera? Get used to putting yourself on tape at home or with actor friends so that you see what works and what doesn't. More on that later.

You should also take commercial classes and workshops, or work with an acting coach who has commercial experience and expertise, because the technique for acting in some commercial work can be very specific and different from theatrical work. For example, it's not often in theatrical work that you're looking directly into the camera and talking to the viewer, referred to as "breaking the fourth wall." It's also not common for a theatrical project to be about a product or service, which is why it can be so jarring to see product placement in film and TV. Sometimes in commercials, the actors are just human props to populate the world of the product or brand. In some commercial jobs, you will need to know how to work with a teleprompter or ear-prompter. It's not often you will have to use one of these, but it is helpful, sometimes essential, in those cases when there is too much dialogue to memorize it all or you just don't have the time to do so.

Teleprompters project the copy (the words) on a screen in front of the camera lens so that you can read it and still look like you're looking into the camera. Doing that and still being a good actor takes practice. An ear-prompter is weird and takes a lot of practice to get right. You basically pre-record all the dialogue on a recording device and then play it back to an earpiece worn during performance, just repeating the dialogue as you hear it. To get an idea what it's like, listen to talk radio and try repeating everything you hear, right after it's said, delivered in the same way. It's hard to do it right without your eyes glazing over or stumbling over the words.

Bottom line: If you don't know how to act, you're not an actor. If you want to exponentially increase the likelihood that you'll book work, commercially or otherwise, learn how to act. It just doesn't seem worth the time and expense to audition if you don't train and get yourself in a place where you're doing the best you possibly can. Consistent training is crucial for agents and managers to see that you're working hard at being the most successful actor you can be.

IMPROV

A few of the best-known places to get improv training are Upright Citizens Brigade, The Groundlings, Improv Olympics, and Second City. Do your research about each and their specialty. Some teach improv with a focus on sketch writing and creating characters like *Saturday Night Live*. Others focus on improv games, team play, and just creating in the moment. You'll have to try each out and go to the one that you think best aligns with your development goals.

SCENE STUDY

There are so many acting teachers and studios, and people's experiences with them are so varied, that it's very subjective and difficult to recommend anyone. Plus, I don't want to offend any of them based on which I chose to include or omit, and I can't list them all. You'll need to ask me in person for my opinion on those with which I am familiar, and, even then, it will simply be that; one man's opinion.

Every studio works differently, from teaching styles to the learning environment to the curriculum. Some may be more theater-based, using material from plays for the purposes of instruction. Others may focus on TV/film material. Some studios incorporate partnered scene work where you're working with another actor and performing together. Others do it audition-style with you working alone with a reader like an actual audition. Some studios teach specific methodologies, which may work for some people and not at all for others. We're all different, and you need to try things out and see what works for YOU. You may hate a class that others love. In that case, it just might not be for you. Keep searching. But if you've audited every class in LA and are still not satisfied, then you're probably the problem.

The biggest factor affecting your experience in an acting class is the teacher's personality and approach to teaching. At many of the larger studios, you may not actually get to be taught by the teacher whose name is on the door until you're successful or skilled enough to merit it. Instead, you may be placed in a lower- level class taught by someone else who may drastically differ in personality and ability from the teacher whose reputation drew you to the studio in the first place. Sometimes that's actually better. Sometimes it's worse. Regardless, in those cases, you need to determine if it's still worth it to you to study there.

As you audit studios, don't let anyone talk you into signing up before you're ready. There is nothing worse than wasting time or money or getting trained wrong. Find a class where you strongly feel that the teacher is interested in helping you achieve your potential and not just their own ego or vanity. Well-known teachers' names might look good on your resume, but if you don't actually learn how to act, it won't help you in an audition. If you want to be a working actor, the only thing that matters is the quality of your work. And you learn to act by acting, not by listening to an acting teacher drone on and on. If you're not getting up and acting as much as possible in class, consider finding another class.

PROUD PLUG: SHAAN SHARMA ON-CAMERA ACTING STUDIO

I've been teaching four-week commercial workshops for years at Act Now!, a casting director workshop studio in the valley. Many of my students in those workshops wanted to continue to train with me after the workshop was over, so a couple of years ago I started teaching an ongoing, on-camera, scene study acting class where we work on TV and film work, not just commercial. Every great acting studio has its genesis. That was mine.

My goal for the class is simple: to develop my students into skilled, brilliant working actors for TV and film as rapidly as possible. As someone who has studied at and audited a few of the better-known institutions prior to starting my own, I want to walk you through the way I chose to set up my studio so you can compare that with the others and see my reasons for doing so. It will give you advanced insight into the issues that make up the differences between all the various studios as you search for a studio to call home.

AFFORDABILITY

Most studios charge by the month, for usually between $200–400 per month. Some studios let you make up classes you miss. Others don't. Among the reasons they charge by the month is because they are a facility, have associated expenses, and need to have revenue they can count on. Another reason may be to provide additional incentive for students to show up to class since they've already pre-paid for the whole month.

I teach out of my home, so I don't have facility expenses. I make my living from acting and casting work, and only teach because I absolutely love it and am passionate about helping my students succeed. I am free to focus on what's best for their development, not my pocketbook. My students only pay for the classes they attend, and I currently charge $50 per session, whether it's class, audition taping, or private coaching. The life of an actor demands flexibility because our schedules constantly change, so I don't want any of my students to have to pay for a class they couldn't attend and the associated stress. Also, some of my students don't have unlimited financial resources, :) and we may agree that they're ready to get agents by doing showcases, and get in front of casting directors by doing workshops. That may involve them taking a class or two off in a month to use that money to pay for those instead.

SCREENING

Many studios allow anyone to sign up for and attend a class audit, without any form of screening.

For general safety, before I let someone audit our classes I require a phone interview with them. This gives us each the opportunity to learn about each other and discuss their goals and reasons for seeking training. It helps me understand if our class is the right place for them, if they have reasonable expectations ("Can you make me a star?" "...Um...That's not really how it works..."), and assign appropriate material to prepare for the audit. I take a very personal interest in every student, and that makes a huge difference when charting a course for their development. I simply do not allow anyone into the class or to remain in the class if their presence will adversely affect our learning environment.

THE AUDIT

As I mentioned before, some studios charge for their audits. Others don't. At or after the audit, some studios will place you in a class level based solely on your resume and credits. Others will have you perform for them and place you based on what they see. Others still won't require either and just assign you to their beginner class where you work your way up the ranks no matter what your previous level of experience may be.

Auditing our class is free. I think it's important that prospective students feel invited and welcome to see what we do and see how it resonates with them and their goals. I don't need to charge for audits to weed out those who aren't seriously interested in the class, as I accomplish that in the phone interview. As for me, I need to see a prospective student act and observe what they already do well, if anything, and how I would approach their development. Based on our phone interview, I assign material from TV or film that is both appropriate for the types of roles the student would actually audition for and of a kind that will best help me see where they are with the development of their acting process, their approach to the work. After watching the class, feeling welcomed and comfortable, and seeing how I work with the students in the class, auditors then get up and perform their assigned material for the class.

CLASS SIZE
Many studios average 15, 20 or even more students in a three or four hour class, in which case there is only

enough time for each student to get up and work for 15 minutes, if they're lucky. Oftentimes it's much less.

I limit my class size to six and our class usually lasts four hours. That means my students are working for at least 30 minutes in every class. We have time to see what they do on their first take, discuss the scene and their choices, refine them or do re-directs, explore other options, get their performance where it needs to be for them to have gotten what I wanted them to get out of that assigned material, and rehearse that performance to get it in their body and achieve lasting growth.

The only way to learn how to act is by acting. Acting is a physical and experiential craft, not an intellectual one. But my students are not just growing twice as fast as those only getting 15 minutes or less in their classes, as the math would suggest. I would argue that those only getting up for 15 minutes constitutes an incomplete and insufficient learning experience that significantly decreases the rate of growth. The proof is in the pudding. My students are developing at an amazing rate. This kind of growth is only possible when the teacher has the time to really work with their students. I can't tell you how many actors show up at my auditions or in my class who've spent years at other studios missing basic components of their development that are holding them back from achieving competence, confidence and booking work.

CLASS MATERIAL

Some studios use material from plays while others use material from TV and film. They may assign unique material to each student, have the students find and bring in their own material or provide one assignment for the whole class to work on together. Students might get new material every week or work on the same piece for an extended period of time. They might use current material or use material that is years or even decades old. Some offer cold reading training. Some don't. Finally, some studios incorporate acting exercises, meditation, and other activities into their curriculum.

My students want to work in TV and film, not theater, so I believe in developing their skills with the tools they would use in that medium. The writing style and formatting of TV and film material differs greatly from that of plays. I want my students learning the ins, outs, and nuances of all the different formats, genres and writers' voices in TV and film. Every week I give each one a new, unique assignment from TV or film based on whatever area of development we're working on together. I choose material appropriate for their type, that they would actually audition for, so they get experience with the kinds of roles they would actually book and play. I also incorporate current material whenever possible, except when no current material will provide the student with the appropriate challenge or growth opportunity we're focusing on.

In our class, we focus on four activities: audition-style prepared reads, partnered scene work, cold reading and cold cold/frozen reading.

AUDITION-STYLE PREPARED READS

This is what every working actor does every day to audition for and book work. It's just you, the reader (usually the CD), and a camera (except for some pre-reads). Whether in an office or trailer, every day, thousands of actors are getting auditions, working on the material, then going in and auditioning for TV shows and feature films in this format. Actors need to know how to brilliantly prepare and adapt their performance for an on-camera or actor/reader audition. Some readers will try to affect you and participate in the scene with you. Others will try to be neutral so as to not affect the work you prepared.

You have to be prepared for either situation.

PARTNERED SCENE WORK

If you focus on audition-style reads for too long, you can forget what it's like to act with another actor. You don't want the only time you experience acting with another actor, instead of just a reader, to be on set. It's important to balance your prepared-read work with partnered or multiple partner scene work. That's why acting in plays can be a great complement to your on-camera work and training. Plus, acting with other actors is what we all love. It's one of the main reasons we got into acting.

COLD READING

Cold reading refers to when you have to perform a piece when you don't have the time to fully prepare it, which can happen a lot in our fast-moving industry. Scripts are constantly rewritten. You could spend all night preparing for an audition only to arrive the next day to discover that a lot has changed. Cold reading is also a great way to test an actor's skill. A well-trained actor doesn't need to be off-book (memorized) to still deliver a great performance, so it's used at workshops and agency meetings to measure your ability. So many actors dread cold reading and fear any situation where they're not off-book, because they feel disconnected and distracted. Cold reading technique training teaches you the correct way to read a script cold that still allows you to focus, connect and give a great performance.

COLD COLD/FROZEN READING

As the name suggests, with cold cold/frozen reading you're not allowed to read the scene at all prior to performing it. It's the only acting exercise we incorporate into our class, and we do it for a very specific reason. In all our prepared work, be it audition-style, partnered scene work or cold reading, we constantly know how the story is going to play out. We know how it all goes and then have to act the scenes as if we don't know what is going to happen next. We have to forget that we know what will happen next. CCRs force us to live in the not-knowing because we really don't know what will happen next. We get to discover it, with our partner, moment by moment, just as in real life. CCRs are a great counter-balance to the rest of our work that reminds us to be present and let ourselves be affected, moment by moment, by what's happening, by the other actors, and by our character's thoughts.

CLASS ENVIRONMENT

Here is where studios greatly diverge, because each teacher is a different, unique personality who then shapes the culture of their entire studio. Some teachers are loving and encouraging, create safe spaces for actors to take creative risks and flourish, and foster a supportive culture amongst their students, who then genuinely strive to help each other succeed. Other teachers are egomaniacal, vain, and abusive, and create a hostile learning environment where the actors are fearful and just want to please the teacher and not be humiliated in front of the other students. Some teachers take a personal interest in their students and make themselves available to students outside of class. Others take an impersonal approach and are unavailable even inside, let alone outside of class.

Knowing full well that we're all different, I really can't understand why some teachers feel they have a license to be so mean to their students and why those students choose to stay in that environment. I have seen acting teachers talk to students with such disrespect and condescension that it makes my blood boil. These are sensitive artists, for Pete's sake, who've already acknowledged they need guidance by enrolling in your class! How on earth does it help them to hurt them? I think some people just endure it, thinking it's preparing them for the tough, rejection-filled life of an actor, but I don't think that's necessary or even healthy. Sadly, I think some actors view it as a kind of self-flagellation; a deserved punishment for the sin of not being more skilled or successful.

Perhaps these teachers think it fosters a productive competitive environment amongst the students, pushing them to work harder for approval or to out-work each other. That's assuming we all share the perspective that all of us are, in fact, ruthlessly competing with each other for acting work, which isn't true at all. Most of us believe that we have everything to gain from supporting each other and helping each other succeed, because we, ourselves, cannot succeed on our own. We need a strong community of fellow actor friends to rehearse with, create work with and whom we'll hopefully work with on project after project. The industry and this line of work is challenging enough. You shouldn't have to fear your teacher. Class should not be a source of stress and anxiety. Class should be a place to regroup, recharge your spirit and refine your craft, preparing you for the artistic challenges the next week will bring.

That's what I believe, anyway, and I've seen all the proof I need to know which approach is more effective when developing a student. Actors learning in a loving, supportive environment perform better, can focus on the craft instead of politics, aren't afraid to experiment and take creative risks, are more open to, and accepting of, notes and feedback, and have a better work ethic because they're not punished for trying hard and still falling short of expectations. They know there is always more to learn. They pick themselves up and fearlessly engage the next challenge, knowing they have the full love and support of their class family. Nothing makes me or our students more proud than to see one of our own succeed.

As a working actor myself, I've been down the path that many of my students are on. I've made mistakes. I've had to learn how things actually work; separate the real from the bullshit. Then, in casting, I've seen how our industry leaders think about things. All of it has helped me get on the right path, a path which many actors, sadly, never find. I couldn't stand by and watch my students make amateur mistakes. All of them know I am available to help them do the right things and avoid making costly mistakes; mistakes that cost me and others years before we figured it out. It's simple, now, really. First, we make sure they have a solid foundation with their housing and income so that they can afford to train consistently. Then, they focus on their training. When they're ready, and we'll both know when they're ready, we get them great headshots, properly planned and executed for maximum effectiveness. Then we get them going with the online casting services so they can start submitting themselves for work and into the right CD workshops and agent showcases. Once they're represented, they're free to bring in and work on audition material in class instead of the assigned material. Meanwhile, we keep refining their skill with all the genre specializations, like single-camera comedy, multi-cam comedy, drama, dramedy, procedural, medical and commercial or specific types of content, like sexual, tragic or violent. Speaking of that:

CURRICULUM
Many studios have a set curriculum that the students must follow.

I'm here for my students, ready to work on whatever type of work they want to focus on. I have my plan for their development, but if they feel a pressing desire to shift focus to something specific, we do that. That flexibility allows my students to take control of their education whenever they want to prioritize development of a certain skill. I also think it helps us avoid the monotony that sets in with other classes where it's the same old rinse and repeat, class after class, month after month. At the end of every class, I ask each student what they want to work on next. Either they tell me or ask me to choose whatever I think is best.

ON-CAMERA
Some studios and classes include on-camera work, where they record the performance on tape and give students the opportunity to watch themselves and learn from their work. However, most studios don't, or it's an occasional thing, not a core part of their training.

If you want to act on-camera, you need to know how your work looks on-camera. There was good acting before there were on-camera acting classes, but now that these tools are available to us, they give us the opportunity to develop our craft much more quickly and specifically. We can instantly see what's working and what isn't. We can calibrate our performances so that we know that our choices are showing up as intended in our audition tapes. We know what the CD's are going to see when watching our audition. Auditions are essential for booking work in TV and film and they are on tape, so we have to hone our acting skills *and* our auditioning skills, which include on-camera work.

I think maybe some studios don't include on-camera work as part of their curriculum because they're old school or don't have the technical know-how to include it. That's a benefit of working with a teacher who has experience with technology and behind the camera in casting, not just acting. Regardless, not only do we tape the work in class, each of my students has a private, shared online folder where I post their work from class for the student's review. All of my students can go back at any time and see all the work they've done in class since they started and how their scenes evolved from the first take to the last and witness how they've grown as artists from their first class to their most recent.

PRESSURE TO SIGN UP

Many studios pressure auditing students to sign up on the spot. They assume that if you're there auditing, you must be interested in signing up, so it isn't necessarily unreasonable for them to try to lock you in. However, some will act offended or as if you wasted their time if you don't sign on the dotted line and accept their "invitation" to join the studio.

I'm completely opposed to putting people on the spot and pressuring them. I don't believe in making people feel bad about not buying your product. If your product is good, people will see the value in it and choose to buy it on their own. I welcome actors to audit my classes and at the end of the night, no matter how enthusiastic they may be about joining our class, I tell them to sleep on it and audit other classes so they have a frame of reference for how my class differs from others. I want people to make a clear-headed decision. I want students who really value the way I teach and the way our class works. I want people to know it was their own choice to be with us, because that is an empowered place from which to approach class, whereas others feel suckered in or taken advantage of if they were pressured to make an impulse decision. I only want students in my class who really want to be there, who have made a commitment to their own development with the support of my guidance.

END OF ACTING STUDIOS PRIMER

That should give you a real working knowledge of how to evaluate the kind of class experience you want for yourself and what to expect. You'll know what to pay attention to when you're doing your audits. And you're welcome to audit our class anytime. Visit shaansharma.com for more information and call me at 310-531-8986 to have our fun phone interview. I also teach a four-week commercial workshop each month. They're every Monday night for four weeks beginning the first Monday of each month. Contact me to be added to the waiting list.

FREE, BASIC, FUNDAMENTAL ACTING TIP

You are enough. Just as you are. Seriously. Even experienced actors struggle with this. Acting is not about reinventing yourself with every role. Don't create a "character" from scratch unless the role is really that specific. You are already a character, one that is vibrant and unique and fully fleshed out. Just come in and be yourself. You are interesting enough and entertaining enough just as you are. Much of commercial acting is just being a normal, easy-going person enjoying a product or service. Trust that you are enough. Just relax. Many actors ask how they are supposed to differentiate themselves and stand out when we see so many people for the same role. My answer is always the same. Be yourself. There is only one you. Only you see the world as you do, laugh the way you do, walk and talk the way you do. You have a unique voice and mannerisms. Don't cover up all that individuality by turning yourself into a generic, cardboard cut-out of what you think will impress the clients. That's what amateur actors do. Just listen to us, be yourself, do your best, and have fun.

CHAPTER FIVE
Pix or you don't exist.
Headshots, Glorious Headshots.

Virtually all commercial casting is done online using online services. The two main services used here in Los Angeles are Casting Networks and Casting Frontier. More on them in the next chapter.

An agent can't submit you for jobs and get you auditions

unless the casting director can see what you look like. You'll need photos for that, at least one good one. For commercial work, sometimes it helps to have a variety because not every CD will instinctively know that you will look good cleaned up in a suit if your main headshot is of you in a leather vest with scruff and tousled hair.

Since you've already examined your look in detail and decided on what type(s) you are and what roles you'd go in for, it's time to capture that on camera. There are a billion headshot photographers out there, and you will spend a couple hundred to over a thousand bucks. Just do some research, check out their work, get recommendations from people in the industry, and make sure you feel comfortable that they are going to help capture the best of you. If a photographer is asking a lot of questions about what you want, that's a good sign. If they sound like they know what types of looks will help you get the best results, how you should dress and be styled hair and make-up-wise, that's also a good sign. If they're just really good liars, well then . . . shit. Just do your research and try to meet with any who interest you if you can for a consultation where you can ask all the important questions and plan ahead.

My headshot photographers are Theo (pronounced tee-oh) and Juliet (pronounced jew-lee-eht). Look 'em up. Their studio is one of the best in the business, and unsurprisingly, also one of the most expensive, but your headshot is your main marketing tool so it's worth it to do it right. I've sent many friends and students to them, and they're never disappointed. Just be forewarned that they book two to three months out, so don't call and harass them, expecting to get in right away.

The most important thing we in casting need from your headshot is that it looks like you and we can clearly see your face and hair. If you have black hair, try not to have a black background, and other obvious examples. Those of you who've dabbled in online dating must know that people's pictures can be deceiving. That defeats the purpose of your photos for us as well, so don't do it. Make sure it looks like you on a good day with your tooth brushed.

When you or your agent submits your photos online to casting, they will show up on our computer screens as small images slightly bigger than a postage stamp. Make sure the photo is of your head (hence HEADSHOT) or cropped or zoomed in where we can see your face and eyes. If we can't connect with you instantly, it will be too easy to move to the next actor's photo. Save your full-length modeling photos for Model Mayhem or Explore Talent.

The two biggest categories of roles are casual, and business. Having at least one photo as a business professional and one as you would normally rock it on a weekend is a good place to start. Some people get crazy with it and get multiple looks: me as a construction worker, me as a doctor, me as a gay hairdresser, me as a military commando, etc. While I personally think that's hilarious and awesome, you don't need it. Just make sure you're smiling in your commercial headshots so we can see if you have teeth, and if so, that they're reasonably straight. Sorry to any readers who have snaggleteeth. I'm sure someone will make another fantasy movie and need people like you to play orcs.

During your shoot, I highly recommend channeling the vibe of the role or look you're doing at that moment. If you're doing your young dad look, think things at the camera, like "Hi! You look great today. So nice to see you." If you're in your suit for a more professional look, maybe think things like "I'm on it, boss. No problem. You're in good hands. Come on in and have a seat." Whatever your acting process is, if you even have one yet, just make sure you're alive, fresh, and vibrant so that your photos don't look boring and stale, full of vacant, fake smiles. If you don't know how to do that, you'd better have chosen a photographer that knows how to pull it out of you.

After it's all done, you've gotten your photos back and chosen one or two of the best ones, it's time to assemble headshots, or pic/resumes. Basically, get 8x10 duplicates made of your best headshot photo with your name printed somewhere on the front, preferably not covering your face. Then, on the back, you print or attach a cut-down-to-fit resume that should include your name, union status, stats like height and weight, and your TV/film/theater credits, training, special skills, etc.

Do NOT list the commercial work you've done. Just put "conflicts available upon request." You don't want people to dismiss you because of a job you did for a competitor a long time ago. There may no longer be a conflict issue, but they may not understand that at first glance, especially because they might not want someone who has worked for a competitor at any time in the past. Let your agent manage that situation. (I'll be discussing conflicts in more detail in a later chapter.)

I've attached a sample resume at the end of this book for you to check out. While most commercial casting is done electronically, there will still be the odd occasion when you will need to have a headshot with you, especially at a callback when some directors want to see what other work you've done. Also, many TV and film directors direct commercials in between jobs to make ends meet. Being prepared with your headshot could lead to an opportunity in their next theatrical project. Of course, at virtually all theatrical castings they will want a headshot from you.

Bottom line: Make headshots and have them with you at all times.

CHAPTER SIX
We don't take headshots.
Online casting services you need to use.

Almost all commercial casting directors now use online casting services to put out breakdowns. "Breakdowns" list the jobs and roles they are casting, along with whatever relevant details they can provide. Agents receive these breakdowns and can submit their actors to casting electronically right through the same system. CD's then decide on whom to schedule for an audition and send times out to those actors' agents. That's when you get the call/text/email from your agent letting you know you have an audition. You need to be there. It's hard enough to get you an audition; if you don't or can't make it to them, you probably won't have an agent for long. Besides, isn't that what you've always wanted? An AUDITION?? A chance to be discovered and celebrated for the star you know you are? Get there, dumbo. Or don't act.

Commercially, you need to sign up for and maintain your account on Casting Networks and Casting Frontier. Make sure to completely fill out your profile and upload current photos. On the theatrical side, there's also Actors Access, the actor portal into the Breakdown Services system, the main online casting service used by TV/film CD's, and also Now Casting, but the breakdowns visible to the general public are usually for low budget and student films, or really hard to find roles like one-legged Asian opera singers.

The cool thing about these online services is that when you come into an audition, we often don't need your headshot because we already have access to all the photos and information from your online profile. Within moments of leaving the room, your audition is posted online for the clients to see, along with all your profile information. It saves time, paper, and money. It's awesome. But if your profile is incomplete, you look like a lazy/clueless asshole, so don't be that guy/girl. Fill out your profiles completely. Completely completely. Pay particular attention to the special skills section where you can list all the different specific skills you have and activities you do, like sports, art forms, musical talents, even weird stuff like being able to touch your nose with your tongue or raise one eyebrow. Sometimes, casting needs something that specific and searches the online database using those keywords. But DON'T LIE or over-exaggerate what you can do. If you say you play piano, you'd better be able to back it up, or you just wasted everyone's time.

On that note, here are some common traps you may fall into when taking stock of who you are while filling out your online profiles. Let's fix it before you even start:

USERNAME AND PASSWORD

Know this shit. Period. No one cares when you can't remember how to log into *your own account*. You know your Facebook, Grindr, or Tinder login info so we know you can do it if you really care. You'll just look like a technologically inept and clueless bunghole. Put the info in your phone so you don't forget.

AGE RANGE

Keep this to a five-year span. If you are 25, don't put 18–30, put 22–27. If you look on the younger side, then maybe 21–26. We all want to be young forever or be eligible for as much work as possible, but you're making our job much harder if we're casting for high school teens and a 30-year-old shows up. Awkward.

CREDITS

As you'll see in the Sample Resume attached at the end of this book, the only TV credits that matter and should be listed are co-star, guest-star, and series regular. Do not list extra or featured. Just because we saw your face for a second doesn't mean you can act. Only booking co-star roles and above count. For film, you're either an under-five, supporting, or lead; it's the same kind of tiered role classification.

TRAINING

Only list studios or courses that made a significant impact on your development and skill as an actor. If you only audited a class or took it for one month and didn't learn anything, it doesn't make sense to give yourself or the studio credit. If you took an amazing on-camera or commercial workshop that transformed the way you work, that is much more important to list. Do not list casting director workshops or showcases here.

ACCENTS AND DIALECTS

Unless you can fool someone who is actually from the place, don't list it as an accent or dialect. It will be a huge waste of everyone's time if you show up thinking you can do an Aussie, British, or Indian accent, and you are obviously a hack. You will just come off as a liar. You're here to do *professional* acting work, not more high school theater.

SPECIAL SKILLS

By now you should be sensing a theme with this advice: Don't lie. It is only helpful to list a skill in which you can actually demonstrate competency. Anyone can say they play basketball, but if we're searching for people with basketball experience, we're expecting someone who played on a team in high school, college, semi-pro, or pro, or possesses the equivalent in demonstrable skill.

Bottom line: Though you may resist it, the truth is that the more focused and accurate your profile is, the more we can trust it and the more we can use you. If you say you can do everything, we know that is not true, but if you just say you play the cello and can handle firearms, we're assuming that you showed some restraint and only put what you know you can do, so we will call you in with more confidence.

Some of these online services cost money. Some are free for basic accounts or represented talent. Don't go overboard. Pay for whatever features make sense to you, but don't feel like you have to pay for all of them. Whatever you do pay for, you'll just have to accept it as part of the cost of being an actor in the commercial side of the business.

What the heck do the online casting services actually do?

Well, here's how things worked *before* online casting services:

You would make lots and lots of copies of your headshot and keep your agents stocked up with them. Your agents would then courier packages of headshots all over town to submit their talent for castings. Casting directors would have to look through all those packages at all those headshots and choose which actors to call in, and then call each agency to invite their actors to the casting session. Then, the agents had to try to reach each of their actors who got called in, and if the agent didn't reach you, they had to leave a message *on your answering machine or page you.*

Craziness. You then had to call your agents back to tell them you're good to go. Then, you would get your ass to the audition at the appointed time (without GPS, by the way, but by using an actual, physical *map*) where you would have to fill out a size sheet by hand with your contact info and sizes, etc., and casting would take a polaroid photo of you to be able to show clients what you really look like in the flesh. Then, you would walk into your audition studio where they would capture your audition *on tape. Actual tape.* After you left, casting would have to make copies of the physical tape and send them out across the city or country to production so they could review the session. The whole process would repeat itself for the callback, after which the poor camera operator would have to do a manual tape-to-tape edit, which took *forever,* and then make copies and finally send them out.

In other words, the casting process was filled with many more incredibly inefficient and tedious to-dos, which really slowed the process down.

Enter technology.

Now it works like this, thanks to the online casting services:

You get copies of your headshots made up for those rare circumstances that someone on the commercial side actually wants one from you, which will be *very* rare. Instead, you just go online, create and manage your profile on these casting service websites. When you get an agent, you give them permission to submit your profile to casting. Casting directors write up breakdowns and post them online on these casting services sites for the agents to see. Agents do a quick online search of all their talent in the system to find those who meet the role specs. With a few clicks, they submit all their relevant talent to casting. Seconds later, casting receives the submissions, reviews them, and with a few clicks chooses and schedules actors for the session. The system lets both the agent and the actor know they have an audition via the site through email and text. You can confirm the audition the same way.

You then show up to the audition not needing to fill anything out because we already have access to your online profile. In the studio, we connect the camera to a computer and use special software to take a digital day-of photo, record the auditions, and build a special job-specific webpage with everyone's audition videos, photos, and links to their profiles, which we send to production at the end of the day. They can review the session on their computers or mobile devices the moment we send them the link. They can make selections as they watch and send their selects to casting moments later. Casting sends the callback notices out to the agents to schedule the actors who've been called back. After the callback, editing is a breeze—simply chopping up and stitching together movie files on the computer. We build another webpage with those edits; and you book work. It's unreal. It's so great.

And *still* way too many actors act like it's *so hard* to keep their profiles complete and updated. We have it *so* easy now, and some actors still don't even *respect* it.

Give major props to Casting Networks, Casting Frontier, and the others for making all of our lives so much easier, more productive, more cost-effective, and less wasteful. They have revolutionized our business and the way casting is done worldwide. They are our heroes, and we almost couldn't go back to the way things were before them. We depend on their technology for our livelihood. MUCH LOVE.

CHAPTER SEVEN
No auditions for you! Why you need an agent and how to get one.
Also, managers.

In order to book work, you need to get auditions. There are only so many opportunities to submit yourself for auditions. Most of the best work is only available to actors with agents, because most of the casting breakdowns only go out to registered agents. To even be considered, you need to be represented.

There are a quarter-million actors in town. All of them want to be auditioning as much as possible. But it's obviously impossible to see them all. On an average day of casting, we might see 50–100 people for one commercial role. To have a prayer of being one of those, you need a good agent that the casting directors like and/or trust plus a passable to amazing headshot and resume.

The agents also handle what you don't know how to do or shouldn't do. They submit you for castings to try to get you auditions, pitch you to CD's, negotiate on your behalf, and make sure you get paid. They get paid a commission off the work they get you, so they only get paid if you do. That means they have an incentive to make sure you're working as much as possible, and if you're not backing them up by doing everything you can to be the best actor you can be, you're letting them and yourself down. Help them help you. Help *them* help *you*. HELP THEM HELP YOU!

Managers are defined a little more loosely than agents, who are strictly governed by California law. Anyone can call himself or herself a manager and charge you whatever they can negotiate with you. However, a "manager" is not allowed to make the deal or negotiate with casting or production in regard to your booking, rates, usage, etc. Only your agent can do that. But while an agent is all about getting you auditions and making money off your bookings, the ideal definition of a manager is someone who guides you and helps you develop over the course of your career. A manager is the one to help you choose the right agents, the right training, headshot photographer, skills to develop, networking, support, etc. But some managers get licensed as agents as well, enabling them to act as a kind of manager/agent hybrid but not technically an agent. As far as I am concerned, the more people on my team helping me become successful, the better. I'm all for it, as long as they are legit and bring real value to my team.

Agents and managers find their clients in many ways, but you really only have three ways to get them to represent you: mass mailings, showcases, and referrals.

MASS MAILINGS
Stores like Samuel French, among others, carry constantly updated industry directories, including CD's, agents, and managers. Casting Networks has a link on their website to download print-ready address labels for most of the commercial agencies. However you procure them, you'll need a list of all the agents,

hopefully one that's updated so you don't waste time sending packages to closed businesses. Buy large envelopes, like manila ones or the windowed ones where they'll be able to see your headshot through the window without ever opening the package. It saves them time, and that makes them happy, and you want them to associate happiness with your face.

Drop in a headshot with your resume printed, stapled, or pasted to the back and a separate short cover letter telling them who you are, what your experience and skills are, and why you're contacting them. My first mass mailing went out to 125 agencies and 125 managers for a total of 250 targets. I got a dozen calls, met with them all, and signed up with a great manager and theatrical and commercial agents. Hooked on Phonics worked for me! But it also cost me around $500. Plan on spending a couple bucks per mailing, taking into account the cost of the envelopes, postage, and headshot copies.

SHOWCASES
As I'm Indian, and was already union with dozens of jobs under my belt before I arrived in LA, I had a couple of things going in my favor that set me apart from others in my category and helped me get represented from a mass mailing. Not everyone is going to be that fortunate. An agency has to have an opening in their roster

for someone of your race, type, age group, credits, and skill set. When they receive your mailed headshot, it may come to them a week too late or too soon. It's very hit and miss. And it's pretty impersonal, right? I mean, all they're seeing is your photo and a bunch of hopefully not all bullshit words on your cover letter and resume. They don't really have a sense of what you look like in person, or if you can act, or if you're normal and nice. Showcases address these failings of the mailings approach.

Every day, somewhere in LA, there is a showcase being held at a theater or workshop space where agents and managers earn some extra cash by attending and intending or pretending to consider the actors whom they see on stage, performing monologues or scenes, for representation. A typical showcase might have 20-30 actors signed up to perform in front of 5–10 agents and managers and cost you, the actor, around $50–$100. That's pretty pricey compared to mailings, costing you more like $10 an agent vs. $2 if you just mailed them a package. But they get to see you in the flesh doing what is hopefully your best work. If you interest them, they may contact you within a few days of the showcase, or you can always follow up with them as well, email and mail usually being the preferred methods. This approach has also worked for me, but it took eight showcases and another $500 or so. But that was also in pursuit of theatrical representation, which can be a lot more difficult to get.

REFERRALS

OK, you've mailed a couple hundred packages, and you're doing showcases once a week trying to find representation, but still no dice. You're still all alone in this cold, cold world. Well, time to work the personal angle. In almost any acting and improv studio of high repute, there are other actors who will have had more success in this endeavor than you, and already have representation. If you develop friendships with these types of people and they respect your work and professionalism, they may be willing to make a personal introduction and refer you to their agent. That's still no guarantee, but agents respect their talent and know they can be great sources of high quality talent referrals, so most are open to at least considering you. This approach has also worked for me. I started helping a friend rehearse for auditions, and after a couple months she thought I was too good to not have representation. She made an email introduction and within a week, I had a great meeting and a new agent.

Beyond the three ways I've outlined above, of course there are others, like family or personal connections, enough success on your own that agents come to you, love, or lust and other what-have-yous. I can tell you this: If you refined your look, got killer headshots, trained and continue to train, and put up good work, you will find someone legit who will want to represent you . . . probably.

MAKE SURE YOUR REPS KNOW YOUR WORK

If you have an agent or manager that has never seen you act, how can they pitch you to casting and get you in doors? You want your reps to be excited about your skill and talent and know your strengths and be genuinely enthusiastic about you when they call CD's to get you opportunities. Make sure they've seen your work, either in-person or on your reel.

A NOTE ON REELS

Generally, you'll want two types of reels: acting and voiceover. Your acting reel should be short; no one wants to take ten minutes to watch your reel. Edit together footage from your best few projects that show you acting well. If you put bad acting up on your reel, no matter the production values, it *will* work against you, so don't think that having something up, even if terrible, is better than nothing. It's not. Similarly, if you do voiceover, cut together a one-minute reel of snippets of your best work.

As a matter of principle, you should be aware of what media of yours is out there on the internet and try to make sure it's only things that represent you well. That applies to what you post on social media. Either make your accounts private or carefully consider what you post and whom you add as a friend.

CHAPTER EIGHT
Get your sh*t straight, son.
What you need to begin your journey.

Okay! Holy shit! Congrats! You're represented by Boris Not-a-front-for-the-Russian-mob Agency and they say they are submitting you and that you should be getting an audition any month now. You're one step closer to booking work like a real, bona fide professional actor.

Aren't you excited? You should be. And how! But before that first audition rears its head, there are a few things you should do.

"BOOKING OUT"

A good agent will be submitting you, constantly and without your knowledge, for every role and opportunity they think you are right for. Unless you keep them informed about your schedule, they will assume you are available, not only for the day of an audition but also for the callback, fitting, and shoot dates as well. If you know you are not going to be available on one or more coming days for any reason, you need to "book out," which means to tell your agent as soon as possible so that they don't submit you for jobs for which you are not available. Just send them a quick email that says:

"Hi! This is Ugly Buttface. Please book me out on September 8th as well as December 11th-21st due to a series of laser hair removal treatments. PEACE." (You don't always have to tell them why.)

Casting hates it when you've been submitted for a role and scheduled for one of the few prized audition slots, and then you cancel because you had a conflict that your agent didn't know about. Don't be that guy/girl.

SPECIAL NOTE ON TAKING ADVANTAGE OF US

Worse yet is when you go to an audition for a job you know you can't do, just to be seen by the casting director. You might think it's justified because you're "building a relationship" with a particular office or that it won't hurt anyone, but that is selfish and not true. We're not casting a job to "build a relationship" with actors. We have a freakin' job to do and clients to please. Unless your agent has gotten prior approval for you to do so from the CD, you're just robbing our clients of another valid option and another actor of the opportunity. Our jobs do not exist for you to market yourself. They exist for the benefit of our clients. It will reflect POORLY on you and your agent, and even if your audition was good, it will not make up for it. Don't do it.

CAR STUFF

Yes, you will need reliable transportation, as you will be driving a lot, all over a very tall and wide city. There are commercial casting studios stretching from Santa Monica to Glendale, from the valley to Culver City. For that reason, unless you are a savant, you will want your vehicle outfitted with some form of GPS and navigation system, whether in-dash, standalone, or a mobile device like your smartphone. My friend Tristin Rupp swears by Waze, a free real-time traffic app that'll get you where you're trying to go the fastest way possible, including re-routing you en route to avoid delay or accidents. Try it and blame her if you hate it. I would recommend the vehicle also have working AC, as you do not want to show up at your audition awash in sweat, your make-up melting off your formerly perfectly painted face. Find some productive ways to spend the hours in transit, like learning a language, a dialect, or listening to a fun and informative podcast like "Stuff You Should Know." Take good care of your vehicle. If you can't get to auditions, you can't book jobs.

SUPPLIES IN YOUR CAR AND PURSE/MAN-PURSE

Men: Water bottle, lint roller, breath mints or the like, deodorant, hair-doing stuff, shaving kit, lotion in case of dry skin, quarters for parking meters, extra copies of your headshot/resume, and maybe some protein bars or other healthy snacks.

Ladies: All the above plus oh god why don't you just bring everything in those huge bags you girls lug everywhere. Notable amongst everything should be a hair tie. You will need to put your hair up and back down often. You might also want to pack make-up and make-up removal supplies, a strapless bra, heels, flats, and a bikini (for those to whom it applies . . .).

If you want to over-achieve, have a spare casual and professional outfit in the trunk in case you get a last minute 4pm audition in Santa Monica while chowing down on chow mein at Mr. Chow in Beverly Hills at 3pm and you don't have enough time to swing by your $1200, 500 sq. ft. studio apartment in North Hollywood.

HOME STUFF

Have an Internet-connected computer or mobile device and a working printer. You may need to print sides (fancy term for scripts), cover letters, updated resumes, send and receive emails, access the online casting websites to fill out your profiles, and submit yourself and confirm auditions with casting or your agents/managers. Bonus points for knowing how to use it to "leverage social media for enhanced personal brand marketing and networking purposes."*

*Said a smart person somewhere, I'm sure.

I've found that a paper cutter and a glue stick or good stapler with plenty of staples as a backup supply are awesome. You will need to print, cut to size, and attach resumes to your headshots constantly, and having those tools will make it a breeze. Don't be the guy/ girl who shows up with your headshot and resume unattached, with the resume measuring

8.5x11 for your 8x10 headshot. It just makes you look sloppy and unprepared, a turn off for any potential employer, except, maybe, in porn.

TAX STUFF

You need to double check what I'm about to write with a tax professional for the deets, but most, if not all, of the supplies and items you buy for your acting career may be tax-deductible as a business expense. That could include your phone, computer, car, wardrobe, massages, haircuts, lube (networking), etc. AGAIN, run it by someone who went to college, at the least, but I'm pretty sure my tax dude works amazing magic taking into account all the costs I incur in this line of work. I think as long as you only use those things for "acting stuff," it counts.

PRACTICE ON-CAMERA

Have a tripod and video camera of some sort with which to record yourself when you practice and rehearse at home. If you want to act on camera, you need to see what you look like on camera. Yes, yes, yes, we all know that you hate how you look on camera or the sound of your voice or that you can't focus on anything except the little mannerisms you never knew you had that annoy you now that you can see them or whatever. GET OVER IT. Eventually, you will be able to see past all that superficial stuff, focus on your performance, and learn to be constructively critical of yourself. An on-camera actor who doesn't practice and critique himself or herself on-camera is like a chef who doesn't taste his food before sending it out to his customers. You're robbing yourself of a crucial opportunity to hone your performance and quality-check your work.

WARDROBE
Have a wardrobe of commercial-friendly casual and business outfits that are logo- and crazy pattern-free. Need inspiration to know what to get? Watch commercials and buy the types of outfits that those in your category are wearing. A steamer or ironing board and iron are your friend. Red and blue polo shirts and khakis come in handy in case you have to play an employee of, well, everyplace.

The most common categories of wardrobe you'll see on your audition notices will be: Casual, Upscale Casual, Business Casual and Business Professional. You may see slight variations on the language of those, but those are the major buckets. Then there are some of the other occasional ones like Hip Casual, which means whatever the cool kids are wearing these days, or something specific like a team jersey to play a sports fan, beach attire, or a white lab coat to play a doctor or technician.

CASUAL: Whatever you would wear on a normal day running errands or hanging out with friends at Magic Mountain. Something comfortable, like sneakers, jeans and a T-shirt.

UPSCALE CASUAL: This bumps it up a notch to what you would wear to a nice dinner party or restaurant, like nicer jeans or slacks and a button-down shirt with dressier shoes, like hiking sandals with socks.

BUSINESS CASUAL: Let's pretend you had a real office job that paid actual money. This category refers to how you would dress if you wanted to remain employed. Khaki or nice pants, button-down shirt with tie, maybe sleeves rolled up and tie a little loose depending on how casual the office, and dressier shoes.

BUSINESS PROFESSIONAL: Let's say you got a promotion and now had to represent the company at a convention in Las Vegas, this category includes what you would wear during the day when you're trying to impress people before the evening drunken gambling and stripper-chasing would ensue. A business suit with dress shoes, nice tie, nice shirt, moustache, monocle and chained time-piece.

Here are some examples of each major wardrobe bucket modeled by a couple friends/fellow actors.

Let me introduce you to my gorgeous and talented friend Erika Elyse, whom you've likely seen many times on TV and in print without even knowing it, who has graciously agreed to show you her go-to outfits for auditions of each bucket type. She booked 20 commercials last year alone, including spots for Toyota, Dos Equis and Samsung, and auditions as much as *eight times a day*, so it's safe to say she knows a thing or two about auditioning and acting in commercials.

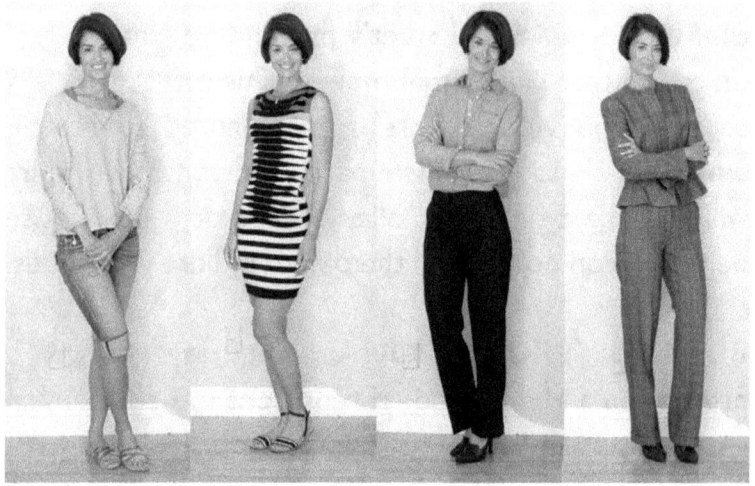

Erika kindly wanted to add: "Shaan's advice inspired me to change my whole audition style and I was able to triple my bookings. Forever grateful."

Next up is the beautiful and brilliant Aurelia Scheppers, whose recent credits include national commercials for

Jeep, Sears, Ross, Volkswagen and Vitamin Water, roles on network TV shows Parenthood, Switched at Birth and The Young & the Restless, and just wrapped shooting the Lifetime feature "Escaping Amish." At Aurelia's age and in her category, she's not going out for Business Professional roles, so it doesn't yet apply.

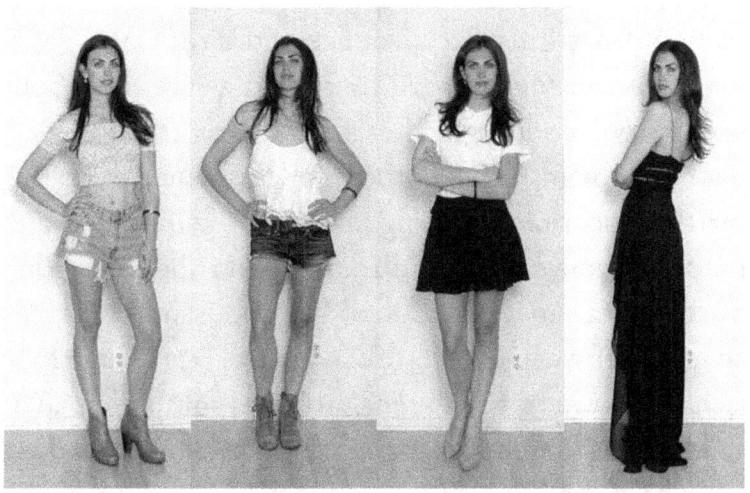

Aurelia kindly wanted to add: "Shaan and I go way back! I have known Shaan since I was 15 years old. He helped me get my start in the industry. My first ever photo shoot was to be the promo model on the posters for Shaan's fashion show Fresh Face Showcase. Shaan is the reason I am living in Los Angeles today, following my "goal". He "discovered" me, if you will, and helped me get into modeling and acting. I respect Shaan so much and am thankful for our friendship. His passion to help others is tireless and selfless. Shaan is truly a role model, amazing actor, session director, friend, all around great person and a wealth of information . . . so . . . take his advice and hopefully you will get the chance to meet him soon, if you don't already know him!"

OMG, Aurelia. I'm tearing up. So, I guess I should mention that I used to produce and direct large fashion shows in Minneapolis to spread awareness about predatory "modeling and career schools" that prey on people's dreams and bilk them for thousands of dollars for their horrible "training programs" and photos and trips and conventions. You know who they are. One of them scammed me out of five thousand dollars as an eighteen-year-old. It took me five years and four fashion shows to get the main Minneapolis newspaper, the Star Tribune, to do a feature on them and expose their operation, which led to them getting shut down. The main reason people fall for these types of scams is because they don't know any better, which is part of the reason I've written this book. It's in my DNA to try to help people avoid making the same costly mistakes that I've made.

I was advised that I should include examples of menswear while I'm at it, so here you go:

To subscribe to Foreign Affairs as well, visit http://www.foreignaffairs.com/.

CHAPTER NINE
OMG!! An audition!
What to do when you get the call/text/ email that you have an audition.

You checked your phone, and you have an email from your agent for an audition! Congrats! Saddle up. It's go time.

First of all, you need to make sure you can even attend the audition. There's no point in auditioning if you can't do the job due to some product or schedule conflict. If you kept your agent informed about any conflicts or booked out dates, you should be good to go, but check the information anyway just to be sure. If you have any conflicts they don't know about, let your agent know right away.

For example, my manager got me an audition for a credit card spot. He didn't know I had a conflict because it was through my commercial agent that I had booked another credit card company spot shortly before. I didn't catch it myself until it was too late when I ended up booking the job but had to turn it down because of the conflict, which was terrible for all parties involved. Learn from my mistake. Do as I say, not as I did. On that note, if you have a manager and an agent both submitting you for auditions, make sure they're in communication with each other about product conflicts and booked out dates to stop what happened to me from happening to you.

If you're good to go on the project and all the dates, read the audition email very carefully. It will contain the job, role breakdown, and all the details. Check the date, location, and time of the audition. Usually, it will be for the next day, but it might be for the same day or for two days from now. As for the location, first calls and callbacks can be at two totally different locations, so don't assume they'll both be at the same studio. Sometimes, a facility is overbooked, and a CD may have to hold a session somewhere other than their home base. Sometimes, clients want to hold the callback at their production company's place or at a studio closer to LAX or one with special amenities. Whatever the reason, it happens a lot, and you don't want to end up having driven all the way across town for no reason and potentially even miss an audition or callback entirely because of it.

After confirming the location, next make sure you are available to attend the audition at the stated scheduled time. If you have a conflict, see if you can change your schedule to make it work. You did not leave Bumblefuck, Idawherever, USA for LA to miss your gosh dang auditions.

You can ask your agent to ask casting for a "time frame," meaning from what time to what time they are seeing your specific role in hopes that they'll let you come anytime during that time frame, giving you more flexibility in making it work with your schedule. Be prepared for the possibility they will not offer time frames. Some casting sessions are planned out very specifically, wanting to see certain actors audition together, so coming early or late would mess that up. If you don't get approved for a time frame and come too early or late anyway, you can have no reasonable expectation of being seen. Sometimes, we can fit you in, but other times, it's too disruptive, or we just don't have the time. Remember, it's a job interview. You wouldn't show up to another job interview at any time other than the appointment time unless you were an airhead or self-sabotage-y or just plain rude. And bear in mind that our lunch break is almost uniformly city-wide from 1–2pm. If you come right at or just after our scheduled break, you may be turned away, asked to wait, or to come back later. Don't bitch about it. It's your fault, not ours, and we be hungry and in need of a much-deserved break.

If you absolutely can't find a way to make an audition work for your schedule, tell your agent so that they can let the casting director know, who can then schedule someone who is actually taking their acting career seriously. Otherwise, if you can make it, confirm! Reply to your agent's email with these two words: "Confirmed! Thanks!"

The audition email will also say what style of wardrobe to wear, usually casual or business. Do yourself and everyone else around you a favor and skip the perfume, cologne, or musk. Also, unless the role specifically calls for accessories, less is more. Lots of bling can be noisy and visually distracting.

The email may provide you with the commercial script or a link to it. It probably wouldn't hurt to take a look at it. They might be providing it to you because you'll have a really wordy or complicated role, and they want to see you at your best, which you won't be able to do if you're not familiar with the material ahead of time, or they may be trying to save time explaining stuff at the audition.

Finally, there may be a note about specific props to bring or skills they need you to demonstrate. It would be a shame if you gave away your lucrative lunch shift to attend the audition, only to lose any chance of booking the job because you didn't bring your bongos, the doing of which was clearly stated in the audition email.

If the job shoots out-of-state and if it is a union job, there are strict rules as to how that gets handled, including compensating you for your travel, meals and accommodations, daily expenses, etc. so you should be A-OK. If it is non-union, however, you'd better be really clear on what they're covering, or you could end up losing money on the job after all those other costs are added up. Don't assume. Ideally, your agent shouldn't even submit you for jobs that don't handle this part well, but just make sure. As for you, you might want to make sure your passport and driver's license are current and that there are no outstanding warrants for your arrest that could prevent you from leaving the state or country. If you're on the Federal No Fly List... yeesh. I dunno. Tell your agent, I guess?

SOCIAL MEDIA WILL GET YOU IN TROUBLE

Just program your brain right now to NEVER POST ABOUT YOUR AUDITIONS UNTIL AFTER THE SPOT/PROJECT HAS AIRED.

Now, I know you're excited and want to share (probably brag about) the news with your "friends" on social media. First off: If they're actors too, they will probably be jelly, wish you hadn't told them, and secretly resent you. Second: Once you put it out there, you can't take it back, and if you do it often enough, it WILL come back to haunt you.

More and more frequently at auditions, you will be asked to sign a Non-Disclosure Agreement (NDA) legally binding you from discussing the project in any way. Companies are competing so intensely these days that any leak of information about their products, plans, ads, or whatever, can have massive consequences for their business, so much so that many companies conduct their casting under false or code names.

Before you even start in this business, try to keep everything to yourself, or at least, don't discuss or post about your auditions or jobs in any public forum, most especially on social media. In theatrical situations, you could ruin the whole season of a show by posting about your role before it airs. Don't do it. No one really cares except, hopefully, your immediate family and your acting coach. Tell them in person or on the phone . . . unless you signed an NDA prohibiting that. (I'm in uncomfortable legal ground here . . . moving on.)

THE COMMERCIAL CASTING CIRCUIT—THE STUDIOS

Almost all your commercial auditions will be at one of the couple dozen main commercial casting facilities in LA. Especially until you really get to know these places and how to get to them from any part of the city, plan a bunch of extra time to get there, find parking, and enough time to prepare before your audition. Most of the time, you will not get the script/sides/boards (as in ad storyboards) ahead of time, so you will need time to look at the material and prepare before you audition.

Once you've parked and gone inside, locate the studio room for your job and sign in. Read any and all material posted there for special instructions or needs. If there is a script/sides/board, read and prepare. Whatever you do, DO NOT KNOCK ON OR OPEN THE STUDIO DOOR, even if the lobby is empty and you think you're missing something. It's a major no-no. You'll probably interrupt someone and ruin a take or disrupt a group explanation in progress, in which case wait until the next one. Someone will be out to assist you when they're ready.

Sometimes, you will be given a group explanation before your audition and other times they will just bring you in to audition and explain everything at that time. Getting there a little early ensures you will have time to get the lowdown. It also gives you time to let go of whatever else may be going on in your life and focus on the task at hand. The last thing you want to feel at an audition is stressed or rushed.

Be mindful of the vibe you emit when you enter the facility. If you come in all mopey or cocky or aloof, it reflects poorly on you. You're being evaluated for the job from the moment you arrive until you've left. If you're weird during any part of the process, we'll notice. It's our job to notice. We have to protect ourselves and our clients from the crazies. Come prepared to be professional, friendly, patient, tolerant, cooperative, generous, charming, and fun.

Don't assume your audition begins and ends with what is captured on camera. You need to understand that everyone at the facility knows each other and works together. Word will spread if you do something uncool. Anyone you meet could be a casting director, client, associate, assistant, or session director. We look like real people, so it's hard to tell us apart.

A WORD ABOUT LOBBY ASSISTANTS
As I mentioned earlier, the job of the lobby assistants is to help the casting go as smoothly and efficiently as possible. They become the buffer between the lobby and the studio. We count on them to keep everything and everyone organized. They keep in close touch with us and with the CD about talent cancellations, role imbalances, informing us if we're running behind and need to pick up the pace, or if turnout is too light and we need to scramble to call in more talent. When they're not doing that, they're calling agents about actors who are late or who haven't confirmed their attendance or for job-specific information. They are on the front lines dealing with you people and are unfortunately the first ones to be treated with impatience, condescension, and flat-out bad or rude behavior.

If you want to work commercially in this town, treat the lobby assistants like gold. They are a cherished part of our team. Like us, many of them work all over, so they're good people to know.

Don't bother them every two seconds asking if it is your turn to audition yet. It's like kids asking, "Are we there yet?" over and over. Signing in is not like taking a ticket at the deli counter. Just because you signed in ahead of someone doesn't necessarily mean we will audition you in that order. We can change the order in which we see people for any number of reasons, usually having to do with putting together groups that make sense, waiting for the right scene partner for you to arrive, or accommodating an actor that has a time constraint. We will do our best to accommodate you on those occasions when you have a time constraint, so be generous and patient as we try to help others. As long as we get you in and out in under an hour, we are doing our job. Sometimes, it feels like every actor is coming up to us, hoping to get in ahead of others because of some pressing "emergency," and we know some of them are just being selfish divas. If you have another audition somewhere, good for you, but it does not entitle you to skip ahead of others at this one. If you didn't have enough time for our audition, you should have declined it. You can have no reasonable expectation that we will be able to accommodate your schedule at the expense of others or our casting. Politely inform the lobby assistant if you have a real urgency, then trust that we'll do the best we can. We love to help, but not if you stress us out about it.

When the lobby assistant greets you and checks you in, he or she may ask which role you were called in for or your assigned audition time. If you don't know the answer to these questions, you will look like a total dipshit. Since the info is in the audition email, we will know that you are one of those clueless wannabes who expect success without doing their job. You wouldn't believe how many people wander around a facility without a clue as to what job and role they're there for. It is your job to be prepared and knowledgeable if you want to be taken seriously and stand a chance of booking work.

Lobby assistants are not free dog, children, or personal item sitters. One moment it may look like they're stuck at the sign-in desk, but at any moment they may be called away and cannot be held accountable for your baggage. They are OUR assistants, not yours.

Finally, in order for lobby assistants to do their job, they need the lobby to be quiet to check people in, put groups together, and call for actors or groups when it's their turn. That brings me to:

SPECIAL NOTE ON TALKING IN STUDIO LOBBIES WHILE WAITING TO AUDITION AND PERSONAL VENTING OPPORTUNITY

I get it. We all get it. It's all very exciting. A bunch of talented and/or pretty people, some of whom you've befriended or wish to befriend, are gathered together to share in the experience of the pursuit of your common passions. You want to flirt, chat, and (vomit in mouth) "network." We get it. Just don't forget that we're recording your auditions here and if you're all talking, the noise will affect our work. Some studio lobbies are more intimate (read: small), so NO TALKY. Some are larger, and you may think your little voice will do no harm. You would be wrong. NO TALKY. Lots of little voices form a cacophony, which slowly rises to the decibel equivalent of a jet engine. Not that this advice is going to change anything. You will still talk, and lobby assistants, casting assistants, camera operators, and session directors will still yell at everyone to be quiet and respect the fact that this is a place of business and that you don't go to your doctor's or dentist's office and make a bunch of noise, so what makes you think this place is any different? Don't make me come out here and yell at you again. Two minutes later, it will be noisy again. This is our lot in life, and we grimace and bear it. But at least now you know that you're a dick for talking and making us try in vain to make you stop. (This is not totally true.

As long as you keep your voice down, you're probably OK. But what inevitably occurs is that whispers becomes normal talking becomes loud talking and laughter, which A. is now way too loud all together, and B. reminds us that you're having fun while we're slaving away in dark studios with vitamin D deficiencies for most of every beautiful southern California day. THANKS A LOT.)

Now, as for how you should approach the actual auditioning process, drill this phrase into your brain: Listen and don't be annoying. *Listen.* And *don't be annoying.* Now, in more detail:

THE GROUP EXPLANATION
Basically, if we do a group explanation, it's because we want you to know what you need to know to do your best, so that you can make good use of your time by preparing while waiting to audition. The expectation we have is that since we gave you a group explanation, we don't have to waste precious time explaining it all over again when you come in the room. We also have the expectation that you will have used the information we gave you to prepare so that you do a great job, and we don't waste time on needlessly botched takes. In other words, the group explanation makes you better prepared and saves us time.

When you don't listen during the group explanation, it drives us absolutely, face-palmingly, losing-faith-in-humanity mad. There is no excuse for you to not pay attention during the explanation. Get off your stupid phone. Stop sexting. Now is not the time to staple your resume to your headshot that I don't need anyway. Now is the time for you to listen, ask questions, and take our direction on how to give us a performance that will get you booked. If you come in later, and it's clear you're asking basic things that were already explained, it makes us want to physically throw you out of our studio. Since we can't do that, you will see us sigh, with soul-crushing resignation, as we attempt to summon the patience to repeat ourselves for the fifty-bazillionth time, with all the clarity and attention to detail that our job requires. Don't do that to us. Help us help you. Help US help YOU. HELP US HELP YOU!

Consider this: You are a professional auditioner, and sometimes you get to book work. You can't take auditions for granted or look at them like they're a pain in your ass. There are hundreds of thousands of other actors who would love to have an audition. You need to see auditions as the integral part of the acting process that they are. It's not something to be suffered through or an indignity to be endured. You have to be able to demonstrate your skill and professionalism in order to be hired as an actor. The acting requirements can change drastically from job to job so you have to prove yourself again in each new scenario. Take each audition seriously and sooner or later, you will book another job and get to work. Resisting or acting like you're above the audition process is the same thing as resisting and acting like you're above a job interview. You are not better than what you do in an audition. An audition shows us exactly how good you are and how you respond to acting under pressure, which is what a professional set has lots of. So get your head on straight and most important, come ready to listen and not be annoying.

THE STUDIOS

What follows is a list of the most common casting facilities, which casting directors are currently based out of each, as of the time I wrote this (which could have been years ago for all you know), and insider tips on the quirks of each facility, like parking and stuff. For a great parking resource that is much better researched and presented than what follows, visit actorswillbetowed.com. In no particular order:

200 South
200 S La Brea Ave
Los Angeles, CA 90036

Technologies used: Casting Networks' Fast Capture—tied to your castingnetworks.com profile.

HOME TO:
Ross Lacy Casting
Mel and Liz Casting
Petite Casting
Dowd Roman Casting
Spot Casting
Pam Starks Casting
Jeff Rosenman Casting
Spitfire Casting

It's above the Petco and Lamps Plus at the corner of 2nd and La Brea. The entrance is on La Brea. It has a sign over the door that clearly states "200 South—A Casting Facility." If you're parked on La Brea after 4pm during the week, you'll be towed and totally screwed, so don't do it. ALWAYS OVERFEED YOUR METER. Always put at least one hour on the meter to make sure you're not panicking when you should be focused on your audition and prep. You can't park in the Petco and Ralphs lot behind the building. They have guards that will shoot you . . . a dirty look and make you move your car. Just don't do it. You can park in the residential streets surrounding the block (READ ALL POSTED SIGNS) for free or at the meters. Beware street cleaning days. They were invented to ticket or tow actors' cars in LA because everyone else hates us for being passionate, talented, and in relentless and courageous pursuit of our dreams. READ ALL POSTED SIGNS. FOR THE LOVE OF GOD READ THOSE DAMN SIGNS. There's also a Casting Networks help desk there in case you just can't quite figure basic 21st century technology out on your own, like cropping a photo or uploading a video. They also have vending machines!

Ocean Park Casting
also known as "Ocean Park" or OPC
2701 Ocean Park Blvd #250
Santa Monica, CA 90405

Technologies used: Casting Frontier's iSession — tied to your castingfrontier.com profile.

Home to:
Joe Blake Casting
Cathi Carlton Casting
RMB Casting
Brigid McBride Casting

Located on the second floor, front side above the west entrance to the building. Yes, there are two entrances, one on the east (that's on your right side if you're looking at the building from the front) and one on the west (yes, that would be your left side, genius). If you park in the parking ramp below the building, you will pay out the poop chute. They do not validate. There is free and metered parking on Ocean Park Blvd., but the best place to park for free is the residential streets southwest of Ocean Park next to Clover Park across the street, but use the crosswalk at the light as you walk up because Santa Monica police love ticketing actors for jaywalking. Do not park in the Clover Park parking lot because that's for families with kids and strollers, not primadonnas like you, and it may be illegal, not sure. There are always cops driving around there looking for miscreants. And yes, you will need a key from the studio manager's office to use the bathrooms, which are located out the far side door down the hall to the right. BRING THE KEY BACK TO THE OFFICE WHEN YOU ARE DONE. WHAT KIND OF MONSTER ARE YOU? A real bonus of this studio is the changing room. Just amble on over to Suite 250B, and you don't even need a key. It's very well appropriated; you'll feel like you're at The Gap! One of the most modern and beautiful facilities in L.A.

Sessions West Studios
2601 Ocean Park Blvd
Santa Monica, CA 90405

Technologies used: Fast Capture

Home to:
Gabrielle Schary Casting

Yes, this place is literally next door to Ocean Park Casting. Don't get the two confused and be the dolt who walks into the wrong facility bothering busy people about why you can't find the studio for the job you're supposed to be auditioning for. You'll need a key for the bathroom, which is located out the door to your left. Usually, a couple keys are hanging in the lobby, so if they're gone, you'll have to wait your turn until they come back or go bang on the bathroom door until someone lets you in. (Just kidding. That's rude.) Don't park in the ramp, unless you want to pay to park in one of the like eight visitor spaces. All the other same parking advice for Ocean Park applies. Oh, and you might be auditioning for a job in studio C with the separate entrance to the left of the main studio entrance. There will be a sign posted out front telling you exactly that, which you will claim you never saw because actors hate and ignore reading anything that isn't clearly, directly pertaining to them. You'll also likely run into Dan, the nicest casting/lobby assistant in the business. Compliment him on his glasses, shorts or facial hair and make his day. And ask him how to watch the sun.

The Casting Lounge
1035 South La Brea Avenue
Los Angeles, CA 90019

Technologies used: Both iSession and Fast Capture—you may need to know your Casting Frontier profile member ID# otherwise known as your "bar code" for when some Cam Ops scan your member number into iSession like you are a bag of groceries. I just ask people to tell me their numbers, and I punch it in. Put your Casting Frontier profile ID# in your phone to always have it accessible. Mine is ID29503. Feel free to just use mine, so I get credit for all of your auditions.

Home to:
Jane Doe Casting
John McCarthy Casting
Pop Casting
Sonnenberg Casting
Lisa Pantone Casting

Again, you can park on La Brea for free until 4pm, after which you will be ticketed and towed, so be mindful of that. There is free street parking on the residential streets surrounding and behind The Casting Lounge, just make sure to read all the posted signs for street cleaning days and hours. And yes, there are actually two bathrooms for your use. Even though one of the doors just looks like a closet door, there is a bathroom in there. They like to put actors on deck on benches in the hallway there, so keep your damn pie hole shut, as it always gets too noisy in that hallway. Since the studios aren't soundproofed, your useless jibber jabber will bleed onto some other poor actor's audition audio. The NO TALKY rule applies to on-deck actors as well. If you see a tall, pretty blonde woman walking around with purpose, it's probably Susan, the owner. Tell her she looks nice today. Seven years later and she still greets me with a hug every day I'm there. Jodi of Sonnenberg Casting will probably sing part of the group explanation.

Casting Underground
also known as "The Underground"
1641 Ivar Ave
Los Angeles, CA 90028

Technologies used: Both iSession and Fast Capture

Home to:
Plaster Casting
Davis/Baddeley Casting
Laurie Records Casting
Lynne Quirion Casting

This facility is in the basement of Hello! production company. Enter off Ivar. You'll need to be buzzed in. Then turn left and go down the stairs to the Underground. This place feels like a safe house/bunker; in the event of a catastrophic event like a zombie apocalypse; keep it in the back of your mind as an emergency shelter. There's metered parking on the street. I don't believe street cleaning affects these meters, but you'll need to double check on that, because I'm too tired to find out tonight. I always park in the lot at Selma and Ivar, but that's because I'm there all day. Remember how I suggested IO West as a great place to study improv? Well, it's right around the corner off Hollywood to the west. Drop by and see a show or check out their classes. Two birds, one stone. Easily accessible bathrooms in the lobby. And yes, a cool, white-haired man with glasses may randomly walk into the studio in the middle of your audition. Don't freak out. He owns the place.

Castaway Studios
8899 Beverly Blvd
West Hollywood, CA 90048

Technologies used: Both Fast Capture and iSession

Home to:
Sobo Casting
Tolley Casparis Casting

Stuart Stone Casting
Digital Dogs Casting
Anissa Williams Casting
M. Casting
Eastside Studios
DB Casting
Deborah Kurtz Casting

Metered parking on Beverly. They have a lot if you wanna pay a few bucks. Free street parking in the residential area behind the building, but yes, check all posted signs for street cleaning and other info. This place has a unique waiting area with little plastic hourglass seats. You'll feel like it's storytime and you're all just waiting for someone to come out and read you The Very Hungry Caterpillar. Bathrooms are out the studio front door to your left, but to gain entry you'll need the SECRET CODE NUMBER that is clearly posted in the lobby for all to see.

Village Casting Studios
725 Arizona Avenue Suite 103
Santa Monica, CA 90401

Technologies used: Fast Capture and iSession

Home to:
Ava Shevitt Casting

Charisse Glenn
Leslie Rhoades
Mimi Webb Miller
Chris Game

There's one shared bathroom in the back by the kitchen, so please ask someone (preferably who works there), if you need to use it. Free 90-minute parking a block away at the Santa Monica Public Library. READ ALL POSTED SIGNS. Metered right out front as well. Please, don't ask them for quarters. It's a casting facility, not a bank. If you park in the ramp below, get ready to empty your wallet. No validation for you. Upside? Troy will make sure you feel warm and welcome every time. Might as well swing by the ocean and dip your toes in the water since it's right there.

Loudmouth Studios
11024 Magnolia Blvd
North Hollywood, CA 91601

Technologies used: Fast Capture

Home to:
Beth Holmes Casting

Brand spanking new location. As of this writing, they still haven't moved in yet. They are very dog and baby friendly, so feel free to bring 'em along. Beth jokes that they are "Beth Holmes Casting, Catering, and Child Care." They share an office with Deedee Bradley (*Switched at Birth*, *Veronica Mars*, etc.), and because she scopes out the lobby all the time, make sure to bring a headshot in with you just in case.

Exclusive Casting Studios
7700 W Sunset Blvd
Los Angeles, CA 90046

Technologies used: Fast Capture

Home to:
Danielle Eskinazi Casting
Michael Sanford Casting
Annie Egian Casting
Melissa Feliciano Casting
Pitch Casting
Julia Kim Casting
Cast Partner
Canvas Casting

There's metered and free residential street parking all around the studio. You might not be able to park on Sunset after 4pm; read all the posted signs. No parking in the studio lot. Upon entering, there are two studios on the first level on your left. Check the lobby

TV monitor to see where you should go. If not on the first level, go up the stairs to the second floor. A couple of nice, easily accessible bathrooms and plenty of high fashion model posters everywhere to make you feel self-conscious about your body. Yes, there is a modeling agency in back. You will see gorgeous models entering and leaving. This is your chance. Don't miss the opportunity of a lifetime. Just smile, say "Hi!" and invite them to lunch at the Chipotle next door. Cheap date!

Broadway Casting Studios
902 Colorado Ave
Santa Monica, CA 90401

Technologies used: Both Fast Capture and iSession

Home to:
Esther Casting
Crash Casting
Yumi Takada Casting

There's metered parking all around, or you can pay to park in their lot. The place is GIGANTIC inside with a couple of nice bathrooms for your convenience in the lobby. They're also doing a lot of construction in the area to make way for the nifty train that's coming, so be careful and read all the signs. When in doubt, don't even drive to your auditions, just hitchhike, walk, bike, or take a cab.

5th Street Studios
1216 5th St.
Santa Monica, CA 90401

Technologies used: Both Fast Capture and iSession, I think. Not sure; as with all information provided here; it's good to double-check for yourself.

Home to:
Kathy Knowles
Pamela Kaplan
Alan McRae and Judy Landau
Casting Brothers — Joshua Rappaport and Alan Kaminsky
A Face in the Crowd Casting/Maryclaire Sweeters

Once again, metered street parking all around. Located on the second floor above something. It has a small obscure entrance with stairs taking you right up to the lobby. No reloading the meter. You have to move your car. Welcome to Santa Monica.

Silver Layne Studios
6660 Santa Monica Blvd
Los Angeles, CA 90038

Technologies used: Fast Capture

Home to:
Shane Casting
Bad Girls Casting

You will need to go through a fence to reach the front entrance. You may think it was put there to keep vagrants and criminals out. Not true. It was put there to keep you out, to prevent you from crashing auditions. No parking on Santa Monica after 4pm, I think, too.

1020 Studios
1020 North Sycamore Avenue
Los Angeles, CA 90038

Technologies used: Fast Capture

Home to:
Alyson Horn Casting
Cindy Estada Casting

Do not attempt to park in their lot. You will be towed immediately. There is free and metered street parking all around. Just like at Sessions West, sometimes you may be directed down a couple doors to the right to an additional studio. This studio also has a zero tolerance policy for tardiness, unpreparedness and ego, so be on time, do your job, and be nice.

310 Casting Studios
2329 Purdue Avenue
Los Angeles, CA 90064

Technologies used: Fast Capture

Home to:
Lisa Fields Casting
Pogo Casting
Taylor Casting
Renita Casting
Berland Casting

Metered street parking all around. No parking in their lot, you naughty minx. A nice bathroom for your use. Parts of the waiting area feel like a mouse maze. Bring cheese.

ASG Casting
4144 Lankershim Boulevard, Suite 202
North Hollywood, CA 91602

Technologies used: Fast Capture

Home to:
ASG Casting

Finding this place, at first, is a lot of fun. You can't see it from Lankershim, but you should probably park there because you're not allowed to park in their lot. There are meters on Lankershim and free street parking on Valley Spring Lane just north of the studio if you can find an open spot. To get to 4144, you need to either walk through 4146's parking garage or the alley by the Italian restaurant, Firenze, and dance studio a little north of there on Lankershim. Head in the front door, go up the stairs, and down the hall to their second floor space. When you see the wood benches, you're there. Bathroom is on the first floor by the entrance and vending machine.

House Casting
855 North Cahuenga
Los Angeles, CA 90038

Technologies used: Fast Capture

Home to:
House Casting

A super modern and sleek facility. I think there is free street parking on Cahuenga. Easily accessible bathrooms for your convenience.

On Your Mark Studios
13425 Ventura Boulevard
Sherman Oaks, CA 91423

Technologies used: Both iSession and Fast Capture

Home to:
Vicki Goggin + Associates Casting
Action Casting/James Levine
Jeff Gerrard Casting
Renita Casting
O'Haver + Company Casting
Susan Turner Casting
Mariko Ballentine Casting
Perdigao Casting
Marisa Pearson Casting
Athlete Source Casting

The studios are on the second floor, one door east of the corner and Remax, so please don't bother the people downstairs.

Zydeco Studios
11317 Ventura Boulevard
Studio City, CA 91604

Technologies used: Fast Capture

Home to:
Francene Selkirk Casting

You're not allowed to park in the *big ass parking lot*. What kind of crispy crap is that? Well, it *is* in a strip mall, so I guess parking is for people with real jobs and who actually have money to spend. So, to the meters on Ventura you shall go. Listen as the clinking sound of what little moolah you have drops into the government parking enforcement receptacle. You, my friend, are living the dream.

Seeker Studios
723 West Broadway
Glendale, CA 91204

Technologies used: Fast Capture

Home to:
Dan Bell Casting

Cool vibe, designed from the ground up for casting. Tons of street parking. Upon entering, check the board to see which studio your job is in. Spacious bathrooms and a water fountain! Why not take this opportunity to refill your water bottle *for free?*

Broad-Cast
7461 Beverly Blvd, 2nd Floor
Los Angeles, CA 90036

Technologies used: Fast Capture

Home to:
Dan Cowan

Find parking in the neighborhood to avoid being pressed for time. Everyone tries to park on the street, but if you're going to do that, make sure you give yourself plenty of meter time. Up the stairs or elevator and go right. If you see a handsome man with two dogs and an English accent walk by, greet him by saying, "Long live the Queen."

Beverly Hills Casting
8200 Wilshire Blvd, Suite 400
Beverly Hills, CA 90211

Technologies used: Fast Capture and iSession.

There's a large parking lot off San Vicente and street parking. Not sure where to go? Ask the first floor receptionist. Restrooms on each floor.

CHAPTER TEN
Shoulder to shoulder:
How to fool us into thinking you actually know what you're doing at an audition.

Now that you know where you're going, where to park, you've signed in, listened to the explanation, and prepped for the audition, it's time to bless us with the honor of your performance.

Before you enter the studio, silence or turn off all your electronic devices. That includes the vibrate on silent function, as it is anything but silent in our quiet studios. I do this by routine after I park on my walk into the facility. You do not want them going off in the middle of your audition. It's EXTREMELY disrespectful, especially if it ruins a take for another actor. You should also leave the sides outside for the next star-of-tomorrow to prep with. We have boards with your dialogue up for you inside.

Here's what to do and expect when you enter the studio to audition:

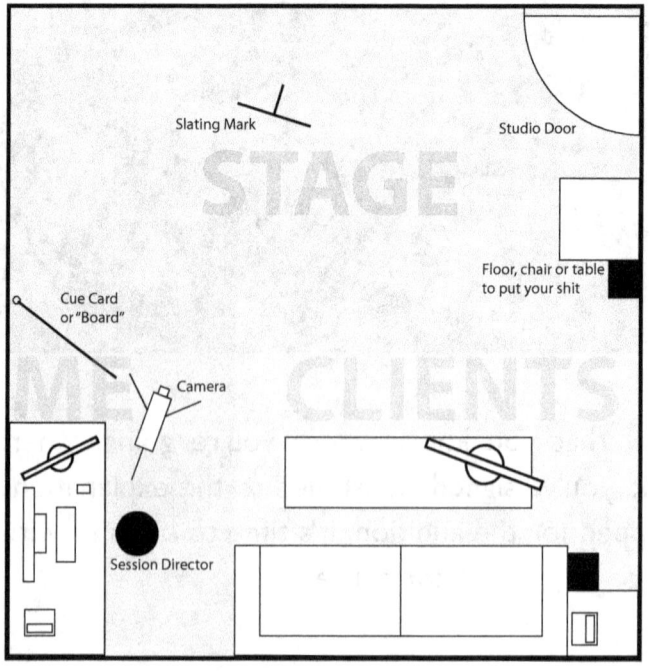

1. **Quickly set your shit down.** There will hopefully be a surface near the door, like a table or chair for you to set down your sunglasses, purse, phone, tablet, phablet, and whatever else. For your benefit and ours, try to keep your stuff by the door. You're less likely to forget it, and it'll save time.

2. **Get into slating position.** There will hopefully be a mark on the floor making it clear where you should stand for the slate. If not, you will be told where to stand. If auditioning with others as a group, stand shoulder-to-shoulder facing the camera on the mark. Even small gaps of space between you take up valuable video frame real estate forcing us to widen our shot, which makes you smaller and our shot shittier, so get close and comfortable with the other actors. It'll all be over soon.

3. **Slate when prompted.** A slate will always include you telling the camera your name. There can be more to it, but just your name is a standard slate. Some of the occasional additions to the slate include:

    - **Special information needed,** like do you have a valid driver's license (for car commercials, for example), or are you allergic to xyz food or product (think make up, cleaning solvents, nuts, and so on).

- **Adult or minor check.** Unless you are a minor, you do not have to tell us your exact age and we can't ask for it, but we can verify that you are over 18 or over 25, the age required for actors to be in alcohol-related product ads.

- **Interview/personality questions.** Sometimes, for part or all of your audition, all we need from you is to get a sense of your personality and get to know you a bit. To do this, we'll ask you things like "What are your plans for the weekend?" "What's one of your guilty pleasures?" and stuff like that. Whatever we ask, don't talk about acting. *We already know you're an actor.* We want to learn more about *you*. Tell us about what else makes you you, something we can hopefully relate to, something interesting or funny or heartfelt. You can't anticipate exactly what you'll be asked, but when you are, try to give us a good answer. And by the way, you're not slating "in character," unless directed. We're actually trying to ascertain if you're cool enough to work with. Just be yourself.

- **Profiles.** This means we want to see what you look like from the sides, and on rare or beauty casting occasions, your backside. When prompted, turn and face one side for a good second or two, holding your long hair clear of your face, neck, and ears. Do the same facing the other way. Then face the camera again.

- **Hands.** Sometimes, we need to see a close up of your hands if they're going to be seen in the spot significantly. When prompted, hold them up and right next to each other IN FRONT OF YOUR FACE. Then turn them so we can see the other side, keeping them together IN FRONT OF YOUR FACE. Then you can drop them back to normal position. We are mainly looking to take note of any scars, missing fingers and tattoos, etc, not necessarily judging you for not having perfectly manicured hands and nails (though you should be taking care of your body, as an actor, hands and nails included.)

- **With or without accessories.** If you're wearing a hat, we may ask you to take it off to be able to see what you look like without it or to see if you have hair. If you're wearing glasses, we may want to see what you'd look like if your vision didn't suck, necessitating panes of curved glass perfectly positioned in front of your eyes to reflect the light from our studio lights, making it impossible to see your eyeballs. Stuff like that. Also scarves, gloves, etc.

- **Facial hair removal willingness check.** We may ask if you are willing to shave your facial hair: your beard or mustache or scruff and whatnot. That doesn't mean you should. The clients will just want to know what latitude they have to clean you up if they prefer or require that for the job. Answer honestly and if you are unwilling, it's helpful to say why. Hopefully, the reason is a good one, like something acting work related.

- **Other.** Dunno. You will be told if there is anything in addition to the things mentioned above. When in doubt and when given no additional instruction, just say your first and last name. That's it. Only amateurs say their name and agency and what role they are "reading" for without being specifically asked to do so. You're in LA now, dum dum. Since you were submitted online, we know who you are, who sent you, and all that stuff already. We only need your name on the slate because the clients will be watching your audition and may not know who you are.

4. **Explanation.** If you didn't already get a group explanation, you can rest assured you will get one now that you're in the room. It may come before or after the slate, but you will be given direction on what we need you to do. LISTEN. The most important thing

in commercial auditioning is listening to what we need you to do and doing that exactly. Remember, this isn't a theatrical audition where it's all about your choices. We've already decided everything we need to see from you, and we're telling you what that is. So do that.

5. **Stand by for action.** Wait for our "Action!" cue, and then start your performance. There may be one or a series of takes. You may or may not get notes/suggestions/redirects to adjust your acting in the following takes. If not, do the same thing with the same choices, just slightly differently to show a little range. If you do get notes, listen to them, get clear about them if there is something you don't understand, and make the adjustment. With experience and training, you'll be able to take and incorporate notes more effectively, but just do your best to make the adjustment. We're trying to help you give us what we need.

6. **Don't bail.** You are not allowed to cut yourself (stop the scene). If you're in the middle of a take and you don't feel like it's going well, or you flub or *think* you've flubbed, don't just stop and ask to start again. Only we get to cut you. If we gave actors the freedom to cut themselves whenever they chose, they would cut every fucking take. You are not qualified to know when to cut. Actors are often hard on

themselves and want to be flawless and perfect on each take, yet oftentimes, our favorite moments are those happy accidents that no one expected. Also, we have no use for bad takes, so if we don't cut you, you have to assume we're getting some value out of what you're doing. Don't bail. It wastes time and ruins perfectly usable takes.

7. **GTFO.** When it's done, say thank you, grab your shit and get out so we can move along efficiently and get the next group going. Otherwise, you might run the risk of:

HURTING MY FEELINGS (some of the facts about this story had to be redacted for reasons you'll have to ask me about in person.)

One time, after an actress finished her audition, she asked me what I thought of her performance. I told her that it was great. It probably was. I can't remember now. But as she exited the studio, she said something like "Whatever. You're probably just one of those losers who won't tell people what they really think." Or something very close to that. Whatever it was, it was incredibly hurtful, and it made me stop my session and walk over to one of the guys who had trained me to run sessions, a total seasoned pro. After I told him what happened, he said, "XXXXXXXX", which means XXXXXXXXXXXXXXXX, which would mean the clients XXXXXXXXXXXXX. It would simply be XXXXXXXX. They would never even XXXXXXXXXXX. "Really?" I asked. "Totally" he said. "If she's that unprofessional and hurtful with you, there's no way we can recommend her to the clients. Her bad behavior would reflect poorly on us, as if we thought she was a good option for them. XXXXXXXXXX." So I did. I took no joy in it, but I got his point.

Months later, I was working at another studio when she came in on a job I was running. Before I auditioned her group, I asked if I could speak with her privately outside the studio room for a second. I told her about the previous incident and that it had hurt my feelings. I told her that I wanted her to know, in case she didn't realize it or mean it. I told her I wanted to be excited to see her instead of worrying and feeling immediately defensive and gearing up to XXXXXXXXX the moment she left the room. I told her I understood that actors can accidentally say all kinds of weird things when they're nervous or insecure or overwhelmed. She remembered and was horrified and apologized profusely. Then we went back in the room and both did our jobs. Her auditions XXXXXXXXXXX after that occasion.

Again, the lesson here is to be very aware of how you treat the men and women that you encounter at a studio. You can't get away with being mean to anyone. We're all a team. We look out for each other and our clients. No one wants to work with an asshole. So don't be one. And if you know that you have a bad habit of saying weird and offensive things when you get nervous, just try to keep your trap shut as much as possible when not acting in the room, and when you're done, GTFO. The 405 misses you. Go be together and make babies.

AUDITION TIPS
Buttons

A "Button" is a term for a verbal or non-verbal way to punctuate the end to a scene. In commercial acting, they're generally improvised as a comedic or fun way to help end the scene well, or make it feel complete, as opposed to awkward silence or waiting for me to cut. It's a way to keep the life alive at the end of the scripted material, giving me a nice place to cut. Here's an example:

FAKE EXAMPLE COMMERCIAL SCRIPT
"Bonerville Hotdogs"

Guy 1 and Guy 2 are tending the grill at a backyard barbeque.

Guy 1:
Is that the last Bonerville Hotdog?

Guy 2:
Yup. They're so juicy and delicious. They've been flying off the grill.

Guy 1 thinks for second, then excitedly points behind Guy 2.

Guy 1:
Look! It's your old crush Rachel Burkowski who recently divorced her hot, successful husband when she realized that she's always actually loved you!

Guy 2 looks. Guys 1 grabs the Bonerville Hotdog and runs in the opposite direction.

END OF SCRIPT

EXAMPLE BUTTONS

At the end, the actors could add a button to keep the scene alive and add a little of their own humor to the piece:

VERBAL EXAMPLE 1:

Guy 1 could exclaim in pain as he grabs the hot hotdog off the grill and runs out of frame (what's visible on camera) juggling it, saying something like, "Ooh! Aah! Yowza! HOT HOT HOT HOT!" and, hearing this, Guy 2 could look back quizzically, look down, notice the missing hotdog and then say something like, ". . . Hey!"

VERBAL EXAMPLE 2:

Guy 2, still looking in the direction where Rachel is supposed to be could say something like, "Where? I don't see her. Behind my mom?" and then look back and wonder where Guy 1 went.

NON-VERBAL EXAMPLE 1:

Guy 2 could hear Guy 1 run off and turn and take off after him.

NON-VERBAL EXAMPLE 2:

Guy 2 could look back, look at the grill, see the missing hotdog and be sad.

Sometimes we will not want you to add a button for whatever reason, but usually it's totally fine and expected that you will put a button on the scene. Here is where your improv training and getting to your audition early to prepare will be a huge help.

TYPES OF COMMERCIAL AUDITIONS
This isn't a complete and totally final list, but a good general guideline list of the buckets most commercial auditions fall into. Acting is storytelling and the stories are as varied as the writer, director and actors want to tell them, so there will always be new experiences.

SUBTLE COMEDY
Most commercials fall into this category, similar to single cam comedies like *The Office*. Normal, real people encountering an odd situation or character and their honest reactions. Generally, you should err on the side of less is more, keep it simple, real and truthful. Don't overact these. You're not the joke. The story is the joke.

BROAD COMEDY
You're the joke. These include the bigger, cheeseball, zany, crazy, extreme characters. Meant to make a big memorable impact. Get ready to go big or go home. Not for the shy or easily embarrassed.

DRAMATIC

Sincere, truthful, touching or informative. Approach it like you would any film or one hour drama.

INTERVIEW

Sometimes all you need to do for an audition is the interview, where you're asked about yourself. It's just an excuse to spend some time looking at you and absorbing your essence, so be short, charming and sweet.

TESTIMONIAL

Sadly, testimonials from supposed real users of a product are often paid actors. Some companies make an effort to find real customers to feature in their commercials, but it's hard to find ones that happen to be good actors and good looking enough. It's you, talking about your experience with a product or service, usually either sincere and heartfelt, relief, or joy.

SPOKESPERSON

Looking right down the barrel of the camera, talking directly to the viewer. Make sure you are clear about who you're talking to and why. Just pretend the camera lens is like a big eyeball of the person you're talking to, because it kinda is, actually.

SPECIAL SKILL

So we need someone who can knit and you have it on your resume. Perfect. Or you can do the splits. Great. Come in and prove it. Very often, people are called in specifically to perform some skill, like a sport, art form, even as simple as speaking another language. Practice your skill and go in ready to do your best.

BEAUTY

These can be for beauty products or services like cosmetics or douches. There can be very particular requirements for how you're supposed to come to one of these auditions. Some clients want you to come with no makeup at all, so they can see your skin as it really is. Some will want you to wear something specific to show your body and form. Other times, you'll want to glam or sexpot it up. Make sure to read your audition notices for these carefully and be ready for an intense slate with close shots of your face and body parts.

BITE AND SMILE

Ah, the old bite 'n' smile. The challenge here is to look natural and happy while eating or drinking, and usually something you probably wouldn't choose to eat and with a smaller bite or sip than you would normally take. Think of food or restaurant commercials where they show happy people eating and enjoying themselves.

Practice eating, drinking, talking and having a good time with a friend or two, you know, for research purposes only.

PARTNER PROBLEMS

If you've been paired up with a partner or put into a group, occasionally you might feel like your partner or group sucked. In some ways, especially in improvisational circumstances, having a dud group can impact your performance. Mostly, though, we can see who's good and who's not good in a group, so DON'T WORRY. Don't ask if you can go again. Don't get frustrated. Don't be mean or condescending to your partner(s). You should know by now, reading this, that oftentimes those you thought sucked are the client's favorites, so don't judge. Just do your best. In some situations, we may actually approach you and ask you to go again with another partner or group if we thought you deserved better. Trust us to do our job. Leave the rest to your deity of choice, if you have one.

USING THE BOARD (THE CUE CARDS)

Fair warning: of all the information in this book, this section and my following advice will not only be one of the most impactful topics that will affect your auditioning, but also one about which there is the most disagreement from office to office, CD to CD and SD to SD. But I'm right. I just am. And you will soon understand why. Chalk it up to another way the theatrical and commercial worlds are so different and the reasons why.

I've already told you what boards are: they are your lines written up on big pieces of paper. They are your cue cards. They are the commercial equivalent of having your sides in your hand at theatrical auditions because you are rarely, if ever, allowed to have your commercial script in-hand in a commercial audition. If you have a brain fart, or aren't off-book memorized, the boards are an essential tool to jog your memory and keep you on track. For union auditions, we are required to have them up for you because we are not allowed to require you to be memorized for the audition. Why? Because that would require you to spend time working on it before your audition for which you are not being compensated. The union has taken the position that if clients or CD's want to require that you memorize the lines, which I and many others see as completely unnecessary for the purpose of analyzing your look, skill, and performance in an audition, you should be paid for that. Think of it another way: Where would it end? If clients or CD's could require you to be memorized, what amount would be reasonable? A few lines? A page? A whole screenplay? What amount of your life is it reasonable for them to demand you spend preparing for their audition knowing only one actor will get the job and receive any compensation?

Ideally, I would be totally cool with you using the board in commercial auditions with me, just like I will always be okay with you having your sides in your hand for a theatrical audition with me, but many commercial CD's and their staff will flat-out tell you to NOT use the board. Here's why:

First, you probably aren't well trained in cold reading. Very few of the actors I meet are. They have no idea how to correctly use their sides or the board in an audition. That almost always results in the performance sucking balls, or at least not being as good as it should have been. It's not hard. Cold reading technique is actually very simple. It just takes practice; not even a lot of practice, but apparently just enough that most actors clearly haven't taken the time to do it.

PROPER COLD READING TECHNIQUE

I can explain the technique here, and I kind of need to in order to make my point about the boards, but just reading this isn't going to make you good at it. You need to practice it and be in a class where this technique is reinforced by your teacher at a granular level. It's the smallest details and errors in your technique that will fuck you up. Nonetheless, here it is:

CONNECT AT THE END OF EVERY THOUGHT OR SENTENCE.
Stay connected when it isn't your line.

There you go. It's that simple. And just about every actor I put on tape every day, no matter how experienced, fucks it up. They try to look at the words mid-sentence or mid-thought (in the case of long sentences that can be broken into parts). They are trying to read ahead and look at their lines when they should be connected and listening to their partner, the reader or the other actors. They are more committed to coming off smooth and picking up their cues than they are to having an experience; one through which we, the audience, can experience the story. The result is a performance that is and looks distracted and scattered. It is less present and more hollow. Many actors end up looking like short-circuiting robots. Why? Because our brains can only do so much at once. Your brain can't be reading your lines and paying attention to the other actors at the same time. Your brain can't make your mouth say words while it's frantically looking between a script/ board and the camera or another actor at the same time. It gets lost, which is exactly what your audition becomes. A lost opportunity.

So, it's no wonder many actors have a real angsty relationship with their sides and the boards. They feel like the words on the page become a distraction and an impediment to feeling and being present and connected to the other actors. Consequently, they resist using the sides and the board. They try to always be fully off-book with everything and tell themselves that their audition can't be great unless they are. I even have actors request that I take the board down or hide it so they can't see the words, because they're afraid it will trip them up, since they worked so hard to memorize everything.

Obviously, I'm not going to argue that performances don't benefit from memorization. They do. But we're not shooting the final spot here. We're casting. We're auditioning many, many actors, all but one of whom will not book the role. Using proper cold reading technique, you *should* be able to give us a great enough audition to determine if you're the right person for the job. Here's where the next part of the problem comes in:

Clients, and even many casting directors, are not actors themselves. They don't know how we make the sausage nor do they care to know. They just want the damn sausage and they want it to be tasty. (Now I'm hungry.) Commercial clients don't care about our union rules, how acting works, or even how brains work, for that matter. Like I said before, commercial clients don't have, or can't afford to have, the same imagination that theatrical clients do. Commercial clients are trying to show the best possible product to their bosses and clients that they can, one that is as close to the final product as possible.

So, for example, one actor, for whom memorization has always been easy, comes in memorized and does a whole commercial monologue perfectly, right down the barrel (into the camera). The client sees that and then calls the CD and demands to know why all the other actors aren't doing the same thing. Of course the other actors don't look as polished as that first asshole, but their performances can still be just as good and useful for the purposes of an audition if they had used the board with proper cold reading technique. But the casting director will rarely argue that point. Instead, they'll come to me and tell me that every actor needs to look into camera the whole time because that's what the client wants. It doesn't matter that we didn't send you the script ahead of time, or that we can't require you to have memorized it even if we did. Now, I've got to tell every actor not to come into my studio until they have memorized their lines, taking all this additional time, all because some producer got one comment from her boss, who knows nothing about acting, wondering why all the actors aren't looking in the camera the whole time. And, I've got to get you in and out in under an hour so the union doesn't penalize the CD for keeping you waiting too long to audition, all for a thing you're not even supposed to, or need to, be doing.

So, because you don't know how to do good cold reading technique, you always try to memorize everything, even though it's not really fair or even necessary for us to expect that of you. Because you *chose* to memorize it all, and because whenever other actors try to use the board, they use it badly, making their performances suck, the clients and CD's have been trained to demand that everyone be memorized and not use the board all the time, which then puts strain on those of you who can't memorize that quickly (we're all different) and me, who is trying to run an efficient session.

So, yes, some CD's and SD's will be okay with you using the board. Others will tell you not to use it. They will even say things like, "If the client sees you looking at the board, they'll just skip past your audition," or other things along the same lines: basically that using the board will make your audition suck, make you look unprepared, and then you won't book the job.

I teach my students how to use correct cold reading technique. I teach my students to love and embrace (literally) the board, to have a positive relationship with it, not a scary one. I teach my students how to give amazing performances, full of connection and depth, while reading the lines right off the page. When you're practiced in it, cold reading technique allows you to relax and put your attention on what really matters: the story, the other actors, and the moment. It's like having a friend with you that always has your back.

So, what are you supposed to do about those that won't let you use the board? Get to your auditions early so you have time to prepare. You should always listen to the CD or SD and do what they say, even if it is unreasonable and non-sensible. Right now, it's a lot of trying to cram square pegs into round holes. It's messy, but somehow the world continues to turn. Most of the time, you don't have many lines or any lines, so it isn't a problem, but sometimes you'll have a ton of copy and it just isn't possible for everyone to memorize it all. IT JUST ISN'T. AMIRITE?

Again, the lack of good acting training leading to sucky performances and the uninformed/unreasonable demands of commercial clients has caused this problem. If every actor used good cold reading technique and all CD's told their clients not to expect memorization until they've actually hired the actor, we wouldn't have this problem. That's why this problem only exists in the commercial world. Theatrical CD's are always okay with you using your sides. They know that busy actors simply don't have time to memorize everything for an audition, nor should they need to if they are good actors. They don't have non-actors breathing down their necks looking for perfection in an AUDITION.

Closing this out, just expect there will be disagreement on this issue. But I have the benefit of working with dozens of CD's, not just one office, so I see how this issue affects actors in all these different studios and I see the variance in attitude about it among CD's and other SD's.

Bottom line: Just be a well trained actor and show up early to your auditions.

Next up is something that I think is so stupid a topic but is still somehow something actors do and ask and worry about. For the love of all that is holy, how is this a "thing" people stress over? Geez:

SHAKING MY HAND

Do not shake my hand. It's not that I don't like you. I'm sure you were raised well, were told to look a person in the eye when they're speaking to you, sit up in your chair at the dinner table, and shake everyone's hand upon meeting them with confidence, but this ain't yo momma's house. Shaking my hand will not make you a better actor. It will not increase your chance of booking the job. All it will do is slow us down and pass me your germs, which will then mingle with all the other germs that were passed to me from handshakers before you until they have all mutated into a supergerm that will make me sick, forcing me to give up a day of work and costing me hundreds of dollars of income; income I need to pay my bills and take care of my (eventual) family. SO when you reach out to shake my hand, know that I don't see it as good manners and professionalism. I see it as an outright assault on my health and well-being (unless you're a little kid, in which case it's too cute to deny, though it will most certainly make me sick, which I will then blame on that one adult who made me shake their hand that day.) (Actually, I never get sick, probably because all the handshaking has bolstered my immune system, but the principle still stands.) It's rude not to shake someone's hand when they offer it to you, and our natural instinct is to shake a hand that has been offered up, but I will resent it because I know I will forget, or not have time, to wash/sanitize my hands each time, and I know I don't want to know where your hairy hands have been, you randy monkey. Just don't put us in that position. Just get your crap, get the hell out of my studio, and go have a wonderful rest of your day, trusting that your performance, if good, was enough to potentially book you the job. And yes, if for some odd reason we or a client or a director initiates a handshake, you should accept it, but don't *you* be the one to break standard protocol.

THE CASCADING HANDSHAKE EFFECT
If one actor tries to shake my hand and I accept it out of politeness, it tends to embolden or obligate the rest of the actors to shake my hand too, perhaps because none of them want to be the one asshole that didn't shake my hand if I am, in fact, a Handshaker, which my acceptance of this first butthole's handshake would apparently indicate. I call this phenomenon the "Cascading Handshake" effect. Just know, from me to you, that if you see an actor initiate a handshake and I accept, I will most certainly appreciate you *not* following suit, and just GTFOing. And now, you too will begin to notice this effect and I hope you'll think of me when you do witness it in the wild.

WARNING! BULLSHIT CASTING
In my first year on the job, I was asked to run camera for a non-union project casting for a new client that turned out to be a reality TV show about how far actors will go, humiliating themselves and being harassed, to book a job. We didn't know what was actually going on until the session started, and they had set up multiple cameras and a green screen, all warning signs that this was not just a casting session. Within a couple hours, I was so outraged by what I was witnessing that I refused to continue working and got into an argument with the "clients" over their unprofessional conduct. The studio I was working at had my back, brought in someone to

take over for me as I refused to work with those clients any further, and made the production clean up their act for the rest of the day. The lesson to be learned here is that you should never do anything that doesn't feel right or appropriate, and you should never let anyone belittle or harass you. If you feel exploited, you are probably being exploited. Walk away. After working with the best of the best in this business, I can tell you that almost all the best people are super nice and awesome, and even the dicks won't cross certain lines to make it a scammy, creepy, horrible experience. Do not do or sign anything that you haven't reviewed or that you feel uncomfortable with. Trust your gut, and stand up for yourself. These guys had found a lot of the actors they called in off Craigslist, another sign that they were only out to exploit those that didn't know better. Don't be so desperate that you are willing to do anything to book a job, no matter the cost to your heart, soul, honor, or dignity.

SIGNING OUT

For your protection, SAG recommends signing out after every union audition, but it's up to you. It's only important if you were kept waiting over an hour to audition, in which case the union will penalize the casting director or clients by making them pay you a nominal fee, like $37 every half hour past the first hour. The hour begins with your scheduled audition time or the time you signed in, whichever is later, and when you sign in, it will ask you for both, so be HONEST. Don't make us send the actual schedule to SAG to prove you're a liar. Understand that the purpose of this rule isn't a way for you to cash in. It's meant to make sure casting respects the actors' time. Personally, I'd only sign out if it was a clearly egregious case of them not respecting your time or running a terribly inefficient ship. A 15-minute grace period is greatly appreciated by casting. If it's a non-union audition, casting will suffer no consequences for making you wait for hours except the ire of you and your agent, which, thankfully, most professional CD's prefer to avoid.

TAKE A "SELFIE"
As much as I hate that word and that practice (I can't see constant selfie-takers as anything but vain, self-involved and/or insecure), I'm not advising you to do so for the purpose of posting it on Facebook/Twitter/Instagram and fishing for compliments. Remember what I said about social media getting you in trouble. No, I'm advising you to take a quick photo of yourself so you can remember what you wore and how you were styled so that if and when you get called back, you will have a record of what you looked like at the first call. More on Callbacks in Chapter 12.

CHAPTER ELEVEN
F*ck! I should have said or done this! Argghh!
What to do and not do after the audition.

Let it go. Just let it go, man. Don't stress. You did what you did, and it was what it was. If you thought you blew it, I'm sure it was better than you thought. If you thought you did great, it probably was great. It's now out of your hands. If you learned something from that audition, great. Take the lesson and do better next time. But don't dwell on it and beat yourself up. You'll be right for some projects and not right for others. It's a numbers game. Just keep doing your job: Show up and do your best, and it will all work out. If you haven't seen Bryan Cranston's Advice to Aspiring Actors video on YouTube, take a moment now to check it out.

Auditioning may be harrowing at first, but it will get emotionally easier with time and experience. The biggest turn-off for directors, clients, and us is when an actor is clearly desperate to book the job. Don't try to force it. Don't come off as needy. Just relax and have fun. People want to work with other cool, relaxed, and fun people. Don't put the kind of pressure on yourself that would make you desperate because we can smell it on you like skunk spray. Set your life up to accommodate the uncertain nature of our business. Booking should always be a pleasant surprise, not a relief.

You'll find that the moment you stop expecting to book anything and just focus on listening, having fun, doing your best, and then leaving and letting it go, is when you turn the corner and start booking like you've never booked before. That's when you'll look and feel like a professional actor and exude the confidence that makes people want to jump your bones . . . I mean work with you. It's all part of the emotional journey that every actor has to go through. Unless you take anti- anxiety meds, smoke weed, or something, I guess. But just focus on doing the stuff in Chapter 17, work hard, and never give up.

Now, if something about you or your audition was right for the project, you'll get invited to:

CHAPTER TWELVE
The (Occasional) Epitome of Awkward: The Callback.

Oh, callbacks. (Heavy sigh.) Okay. What is a callback, and why does it exist?

As I mentioned earlier, your first auditions are sent to all the relevant parties on the client side who then respond with a list of their favorites. That may be one list or many lists coming from the director, ad agency, producers, and/or clients. Those favorites lists are then consolidated, and those actors are called back to audition again, this time in front of some or all of the production and clients, which throws a ton of new and mostly dicey variables into the whole experience from a session director's perspective.

Let me be clear on this point: Most clients are great in the room and with actors. We wouldn't have a job without them. In my job, I work with some of the best in the business, and they are responsible for all the great campaigns we enjoy. Of course, they're coming at the casting from an entirely different point of view than you as the actor or me on the casting side, and even though it doesn't happen that often, I have to prepare you for the potential issues that can arise when people who don't do casting every day and who aren't actors themselves are now in charge of a casting session, directing you and evaluating your performance.

By now you understand that when you come and audition for me, I'm in control of the energy of the room and every facet of your audition experience so that I can make sure everything goes down in the optimal way. When you introduce clients, and usually multiple clients, into the mix, things can get very weird, fast. We have to deal with egos, corporate politics, production issues, and even just a general lack of understanding, sensitivity, and awareness of the etiquette and standard protocol of the acting and auditioning process. If I'm not empowered to help manage it, it's almost a certainty that some things about the callback are not going to be "optimal." Somewhat understandably. It's a big, messy, professional orgy of differing professions, needs, and focuses.

Your agent will notify you if you have been called back to the callback. You will need to confirm your attendance like before; if missing a first-call audition is bad, you REALLY don't want to tell your agent you can't make it to the callback, when you stand a much better chance of booking the job. Make sure you go to the callback looking exactly how you did the first time and ready to perform exactly the same way. That's what got you called back; don't go changing all of that for no reason.

When you get there, be prepared to wait a while to be seen and to be held there long after you audition. You can have no reasonable expectation of expedience, but if it's a union callback, don't worry, you will get compensated if they hold you over an hour, as with the first calls. Why the wait, you ask? Because clients don't work as fast as we do. Because they may have an uneven number of actors for each role called back, or want to see you with another group, mix and match faces, try you with different spouses, children, cohorts, etc. If they hold you, that's usually a good sign that you look or did something right. That, or they had no suitable alternatives.

Be prepared for things to be changed performance-wise. You should go prepared to do what you did the first time, but often, once the director is there in the room, he/she may simplify or otherwise alter what they need to see from you, so stay frosty. Which brings me to:

THE THING THAT FUCKS WITH ACTORS THE MOST IN THE CALLBACK ROOM:
Bad or confusing direction or a total lack of any direction whatsoever.

I'm serious. You need to know that most directors and clients aren't actors themselves. Sometimes they don't know how to speak our language or communicate with you to get you to do what they want to see from you. And I can't do anything to help you because I can't step on the toes of the director or clients, even if it's just to help you make sense of their often cryptic direction or notes. Here's a perfect example:

Let's say you just did a take where the action was this: You enter, as if coming home after a long day of work, hang your coat up, and walk toward the kitchen, ready for dinner.

It's followed by an awkward silence during which the clients are all staring or whispering to each other and looking to the director, who feels he must do something to show his clients, whom he may be meeting for the first time right there at your callback; that he is, in fact, a good director, with a vision, thanks to which their campaign about pizza sauce will be elevated to award-winning heights. He may then speak up and say something like: "Okay. Great. Let's do another . . . So, it's kinda like that feeling when you come home, and your dog comes up to you and you bend down to pet him and he jumps up and licks your face, and your wife has got this big spread of dinner laid out, and your kids run up to you and hug your knees, giggling, you know?" To which you, of course say, "Yes! Copy that! Totally! Love it! Perfect! Thank you!" To which he will say, "So, yeah. It's kinda like that feeling, that moment."

I'll say "Action!" You'll enter, bend down, and pet the air, audibly take a whiff and smile, gazing toward what must be the kitchen to you and then stand and beam looking down as you imagine children showering your knees with love. You then start waddling toward the kitchen, conveying the weight of a fawning, knee-hugging child with every step, a brilliant piece of playful improv, really.

"CUT," I'll say. You look, proudly, toward the back of the room.

How can this be? The clients don't look happy. The director looks perplexed. He thought he was clear, and it must be your fault that you don't understand his direction.

He says, "Okay... you don't actually have to bend down and all that stuff. It's just like you're really, like, hungry and it's been a stressful day at the office, and all of that is weighing on you when you come home, and you can't wait to get to the kitchen to have dinner with your wife and kids. You know what I mean? It's like that moment in your mind when you feel relieved."

I see your eyes glaze over for an instant or like a deer in headlights. You look at me for help. *I can't say anything. I'm so sorry.* You say, once again to the director "Yes! Of course! What was I thinking? I got it! Thank you! Totally!"

"Action!" I'll say, hiding behind my camera to avoid the coming wreck. You enter, looking stressed. You quickly hang your coat up and sigh as you beeline for what must be the kitchen . . . "Cut."

Again, you look to the back of the room. No one is talking. More looking around at each other. Then you hear those two common words that, in that context and within the mind of the actor, almost never mean what they were invented to convey: "Thank you." Which, of course, to us, is code for "Be gone from my presence this instant, you non-star." I watch you leave the room, not sure what to think about what just happened.

And me, understanding really what the clients have been looking for all day would have told you simply, "Can you be happier when you enter? You're glad to be home."

I swear I have seen more actors be judged by the clients and lose jobs for things that were absolutely not their fault but solely due to the poor or unclear direction than *any other factor*. Here are some examples of what I've heard from clients, followed by what I wanted to say in reply:

Client: She was horrible.

My Brain: She was confused because things had changed, and you didn't explain that to her.

Client: He had no range.

My Brain: You didn't ask him to do anything different from take to take, so he understandably kept doing the thing that GOT HIM CALLED BACK in the first place.

Client: He couldn't take direction.

My Brain: He didn't hear what you mumbled at him while he was yelling and screaming as necessitated by the scene.

That's just the tip of the iceberg with regard to what kinds of things can go wrong at a callback. Most of them have nothing to do with you. Clients say weird things to the actors, trying to "relate" or "ease the tension" of the casting process. Actors say weird things to the clients, trying to come off as not-nervous/wigged out or "personable." Most of the time, I see actors get treated really well, but occasionally you're condescended to. It tends to be weirder on days when we're casting pretty people and models, because a lot of normal business people aren't confronted in person by the most beautiful people on the planet every day, so it can be really overwhelming for men or women to sit in judgment of amazing person after person. Apparently, beauty affects the same pleasure center of our brain as chocolate or heroin, I can't remember, the point is, some people's brains turn to mush around hotness, whereas I'm used to it and desensitized to it. That part of my brain has been so over-stimulated and charred that every new person I meet is a Rorschach test.

Be prepared to enter a room full of people who are too busy to care about your performance but who still choose to be in the room anyway, clacking away on their laptops or mobile devices. Don't take it personally. Either they don't know any better or they have bigger fish to fry.

Some people are arrogant dicks and others are super sweet and nice; some are lecherous and others are professional through and through. Until you really start to learn who these people are and get a sense of their personalities, you could be walking into anything, so you have to be ready. With some dicky or arrogant directors, it's best to just shut your mouth, let it all roll off your back, do your job, and leave. With others, they enjoy it when you gracefully and charmingly dish it right back like they're a feisty uncle. Most people are cool, so you won't have to deal with it too often, but in case you do, remember that they don't know you. Don't take it seriously.

Another potential situation you have to be prepared for is that a celebrity may be in the room. Someone you admire. Someone you had no idea was the director or spokesperson for the project. Don't be afraid of them. Treat them like any other actor if you need to perform with them. If they're giving you direction, be a professional and take it the same way you would take it from me in the first audition. Sometimes, we can't tell you ahead of time that they are in the room, for a variety of reasons, or won't tell you so you don't start wigging out while waiting for your turn. Just focus and do your job.

Remember how I told you not to post about your auditions on social media? Now is an especially important time to follow my advice. Sometimes, there are clients sitting in the studio Googling you after you leave the room to see if you posted anything about the project. They are researching you in almost real-time to see if you're a professional or not. No one needs to know you auditioned with XYZ celebrity, especially not this instant. Contain your excitement. Loose lips sink ships.

I teach a handful of strategies to help actors take control of the callback experience and not get fucked by the system as it exists currently, but the best and most universal one I can recommend is: If you are unclear or unsure of anything, ask and get clarity. Do it sweetly, charmingly, politely, but don't risk the job by proceeding while confused. Directors and clients will blame you, not themselves and their direction, for your mistakes.

What some clients don't understand is that you are capable of doing just about anything they require with the right direction, but they don't know how to direct you, so they just settle for what you ultimately just do. They give up on you so quickly, whereas under my direction in the first calls, I usually don't let you leave the room until you've had a win. If it was too hard to get you there, and I know the clients will not be able to get you there at the callback, I almost feel bad for making you look good and putting you and them in that situation. You're not ready or skilled enough on your own, and now you're potentially going to go let everyone down. But it's my job to help you do your best to make the clients happy and feel like they have a lot of great choices. And also so the casting director isn't having a nervous breakdown because the actors they've called in suck balls. Shit rolls downhill. If you're terrible, they'll blame me for not making you do it "right."

That's why training is very important. Sometimes, the responsible thing for me to do is just let you face the consequences of your own actions. That's usually only an issue on non-union casting days when we're working with a lot of newer, greener actors. Union actors are usually more dialed in and capable. Experience and training counts. Go SAG-AFTRA!

So yes, callbacks are a necessary and frightfully uneven part of the casting process, fraught with danger lurking around every corner. And yet, still somehow, it works out and things get done. But at least you can understand why sometimes at callbacks, it seems like no one is having any fun, you have to wait around forever, and leave feeling like you were just in Bizarro Land.

CHAPTER THIRTEEN
The Tease: Avail!
So close . . . and yet so far away.

At the end of the callback comes the deliberation. After we've seen everyone, the clients have their piles of photos of the actors sorted into yeses, noes, and maybes. They'll lay the photos out on a table, floor, or corkboard and discuss who they like and why, who they think looks like a believable cast or family or couple.

They'll figure out if they have enough diversity or too much diversity. Who's too pretty or not pretty enough. Who, in their minds, sucked and who was great. This is when casting directors and associates may be asked to weigh in on the decision. Their depth of knowledge about the actors and the needs of the client can make a huge difference.

After an hour or three, the director and production will have made their selections, called "selects." And they always have to choose "first choices" and then backups in case a bus hits their first choices or their client rejects them.

Whaaa??? "Rejects them?" Oh, yes. Just because you somehow made it through the messy callback process to be named their favorite, their "first-choice," you may still be knocked out of the deliberation when they present the results of the casting process to their client for final approval. Someone at Papa John's thought you looked too unkempt, or too fat, or too much like their ex-wife, and sorry, you've got to go.

In the interim, while production and their clients debate who to finally approve, all the first-choices and backups will be placed in limbo, known as "Avail." It means that casting is informing you and your agents that you are one of the top choices (we won't specify first choice or backup) and are to hold the fitting and shoot dates for us and accept no other work or make any conflicting plans until we release or book you. However, if we release you, you don't get any compensation, even if you had to turn down other work. It's not exactly a fair situation, but one for which actors must be grateful nonetheless.

Sometimes, production will be extra scared of the clients and have more than one backup per role, which means they might have a first choice, a backup, and a second backup. All three will be placed on avail, but only one can and will book it, so the other two will be tantalized with the possibility of a booking and then released back into the wild, like a rejected orphan seeking a new home. But it felt so good to be held in their arms, if only for a moment. It gave them . . . hope.

CHAPTER FOURTEEN
The Orgasm: Booking. YOU booked it? You booked it! Holy shit! You're for realz now!

That's right, campers. Against all odds, out of the 250,000 actors here in LA to act, amidst the 2,000 of you and others like you that were submitted for the role, 100 were called in, including you, and amongst them all, 20 were called back, and after a grueling day of callbacks, with awkward and unclear direction taking its toll on seemingly everyone's spirits, one actor was eventually selected as a first choice—not you, someone they liked *way* more—but YOU were selected as a backup, placed in the fortunate, or possibly unfortunate, avail limbo, and when the client saw you in the selects presentation, you reminded him of his formerly estranged and now sadly long-passed daughter Sandy, and he tearfully resolved then and there that he was going to support you like he failed to support her in life, and if casting you as "Woman A," who will ultimately be seen in the commercial for one second as she smiles at the animated product mascot from across the airplane aisle, could be that first important step in the healing process, whereby Sandy, looking down from the heavens, could maybe find it in her heart to forgive him, but more importantly, that he could one day forgive himself, maybe even love himself again, then that's what he was going to do, and CONGRATU-FUCKING-LATIONS! YOU BOOKED YOUR FIRST NATIONAL COMMERCIAL! You're going to be on TV, make dolla-dolla-bills-y'all, and everyone who said you couldn't do it back home is going to have a bellyache from a tummy full of words. Sweet, sweet validation will soon be yours. Savor it. It may only happen a half-dozen times a year if you're lucky.

What now? Well, your agent will then finalize the deal, compensation, and confirm the fitting and shoot details. "Fitting?" you say? Yes. The Fitting. Someone will call you, or you will somehow be notified that you are to attend a fitting session where you will try on multiple outfits in efforts to settle on the best airplane flirter woman ensemble possible, that says all the right things: Classy, but not unexciting. Bold, but not distracting. Youthful, but not perverse. Casual, but not lazy. Etc. They'll take pictures of you or parade you in front of strangers for approval. Be prepared for everyone to stare at everything but your eyes. They may never acknowledge you, the Star of their project, but never fear. It's not about you. It's about their brand and the message. Respect it and likewise be in silent awe.

The fitting may or may not be paid, depending on if the job is union or not. For union jobs, you will definitely be paid for your time. For non-union, maybe or maybe not, depends on what your agent offered or negotiated. You might also be asked to bring some of your own clothes, so do the laundry, you slob. Or use a laundry service like me. Man, it's great. It really is. I'm telling you. Hoh.

CHAPTER FIFTEEN
The Money Shot: The shoot and life on a commercial set. MAKE IT RAIN.

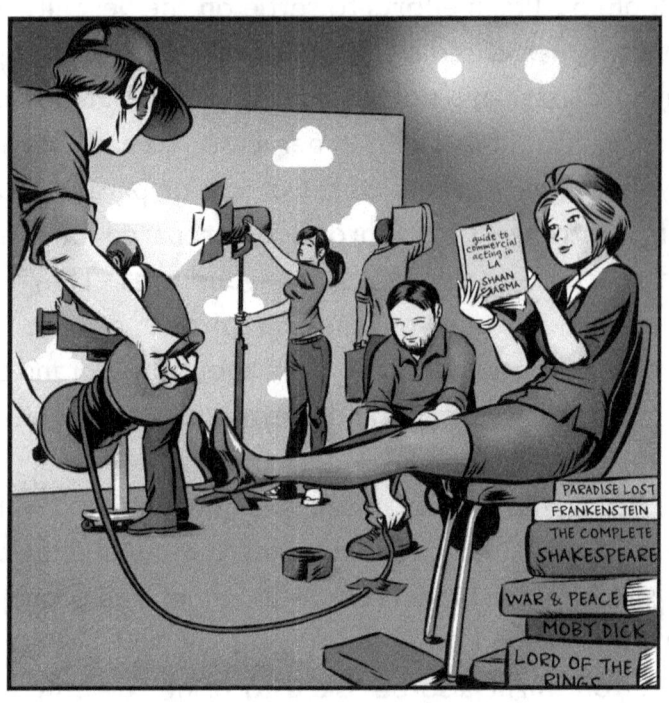

Soon after the fitting day will come the shoot day or days. You will be sent a call sheet with the location, call time, and more information than you will really know what to do with. Call sheets are kind of amazing. If you have any fellow cast members, their names, along with every-freaking-one in the production, will be listed for you to Google away (no one "Bings" anything) and learn about who you will be acting with. It's quite simple really. Show up where you're supposed to be at the time you're supposed to be there. Plan extra time for the trip so that there is no possible way you will be late. You do not want to start your career by stopping it before shooting the one thing you booked.

On that note, before you even arrive on set or location for the shoot, make sure you have your head on straight. Just as in the audition process, the production staff will be evaluating you from the moment you arrive to the moment you drive off (or are picked up by your best friend because you're a scrub.) It is crucially important that you be on your best behavior. Treat everyone with kindness, gratitude, charm, and generosity of spirit. You do not want word to come back that you were a diva on set or an arrogant narcissist. On top of that, be prepared and work your ass off. Sometimes, actors fail to see the big picture and recognize how much is riding on your performance—the success or failure of whole product launches, the gain or loss of lucrative client accounts, etc. People's careers are on the line if this doesn't go well. Focus and have a strong work ethic. No pressure. Just make damn sure that they will not rue the day they booked you on this job . . . and don't forget to relax and have fun too!

Upon arrival, find out where to check in and with whom, usually the second assistant director (2nd AD). Then sit in your trailer or holding area like a toddler on time-out and wait to be told what to do. When they tell you to go to makeup, do it. When they tell you to get dressed in your shooting attire, do that. When they call you to set, go. Easy peasy. Just make sure to keep your bladder and bowels empty as the set can often be a ways away from toilet facilities.

Upon arriving on set, it's now time to work your magic and probably fully realize how much this whole thing is not about you almost at all. It's about the lighting, getting specific shots, and discussions about elements you may never have considered. Things will just take lots and lots of time. Time that you will spend patiently waiting and bonding with your fellow actors, if, hopefully, there are some.

While waiting you will have access to that one holy spot you only heard about in myths and legends: craft service. Sometimes, a snack station. Oftentimes, a spread and feast previously only experienced by emperors and kings and executives at a nice luncheon in a fancy schmancy hotel ballroom. Ah crafty! Candy, breath mints, sodas, juices, yogurt, and so, so much more.

At some point, you will have "lunch." Even if it's at 3am, it will be called "lunch." At the least, you'll have a wonderful, balanced meal. At the most, it will be like a lovechild of the best food trucks in LA and Old Country Buffet with the sole goal of satisfying your most random culinary desires and accommodate even the most stringent dietary restrictions. You will never eat better than on the set of a well-funded national commercial.

But don't eat too much! You still have to act, chubbs! You don't want to have a food baby visible in your first on-camera debut, do you? Just look at all that amazing food you can't have and settle for the next best thing—take photos and post them on Facebook and Instagram to show everyone else in the world what you had access to, and in what must be an ungodly offense to the peoples of starving nations, chose not to eat. You did, however, appreciate it. It's the thought that counts . . . and keeps the calories away! Ayo!

You'll do your brilliant bit of acting, diplomatically navigate the advances of the envious background talent (extras) and engage in brief but charming convo with the clients like a good little networker. When you're all done, they'll say that you're "wrapped," but you can't go yet. You need to be "released," which just means they need to make sure they've got everything they need from you, that you've correctly completed all your homework (paperwork) and signed out. I guess the metaphor those terms attempt to paint is that you're a special little animal wrapped up in gift wrap and then lovingly released back into the wild.

At that point you will rejoin the ranks of the unemployed actors waiting for their next golden ticket. Hope you stuffed some of that crafty in your pockets to enjoy for weeks after as a reminder of your glory days. As has happened to many before you, there's a chance you may never work again, but if you've made a careful study of this material, that will probably not be the case for you. Rest more assured.

CHAPTER SIXTEEN
Free Money! Residuals, re-negotiations, holding fees, and other things you can't control but may pay you tons of money you didn't expect.

If the commercial you booked was a union job, you are going to get residuals, meaning the clients have to pay you every time your commercial plays on network TV, cable TV, online, on mobile devices, etc. They are tracked and paid out every "cycle" of 13 weeks, making four cycles in a year. Sometimes, your agents will be able to negotiate a minimum per cycle known as a "guarantee" that they have to pay you even if they don't run the commercial a lot, because you still now have a conflict with their competitors, also known as "exclusivity," and can't work for those other brands until the "holding period" is up on your current one. As long as the clients keep paying you holding fees, they still have the right to air your commercial, and Ford isn't going to be okay with hiring you for their commercial if you have a Toyota spot on TV right now.

Eventually, the period of being paid holding fees ends, and the clients have to renegotiate the rights of airing your commercial all over again. They can't just keep paying you a holding fee of one session fee (just over $600) every 13 weeks forever and keep you from taking work from their competitors for the rest of your life. That could cost you thousands or hundreds of thousands or even millions of dollars in lost work and income, so they have to pay you something substantial to keep you exclusive in that product category to them and use your two-year-old commercial footage some more. That could result in a nice, unexpected, fat check that you didn't need to do anything for, except still exist. That's pretty sweet.

Potentially say goodbye to all of that guaranteed money if the commercial you did was non-union. Commercials are usually shot with non-union actors specifically so they can avoid having to pay all those associated costs. You will probably be paid a flat rate, either for a specific period of time, or for forever, called "in perpetuity," meaning they have the right to play your commercial whenever, wherever, for the rest of your life, and there's nothing you can do about it because you signed the release. Beware! I know actors who have lost out on huge jobs that would have paid them mountains of cash because they had a conflict with a non-union commercial job they did years ago just to pay the rent.

LONG-ASS SIDE NOTE ABOUT THE UNION, SAG-AFTRA:

When you first start out acting and have no credits (no professional booked jobs or experience to list on your resume), you will not be eligible to join the actors' union SAG-AFTRA (Screen Actors Guild—American Federation of Television and Radio Artists) and enjoy the shelter of their protection, including guaranteed compensation and work conditions. You will be a non- union actor. That means you will not be able to perform in union commercial jobs without the production paying a penalty to the union or successfully justifying to the union why they hired your ass instead of a perfectly capable actor who is already a union member. After making it through that gauntlet and booking a principle role on a union project or three extra roles on union projects, you will be become eligible to join the union, meaning you are not allowed to work any more union jobs, period, until you pay the initiation fee and join. In other words, you got enough experience to join the union, but you're not allowed to take away any more potential jobs from union actors. Join, or piss off and die and stay in the non-union world for all we care. At that moment, you're in a sweet spot where you can join whenever you want and still do non-union work until that next big union-joining job comes along and forces you to switch over. But I must say, there is no better feeling as an on-camera actor than the day you first join the ranks of all the great television and film actors as a union brother or sister. The world is now your oyster, and you can say with pride to others that you are a professionally sanctioned actor. That doesn't mean you're a good actor, per se, but it does mean that you somehow got enough acting experience to get the union to allow you to sully their ranks with your presence, which is, in itself, awesome. And being a union actor also means that you take your profession seriously enough to pay thousands of dollars to join and hundreds of dollars every year to remain a member in good standing. In other words, being a union actor is an indication that you have professional work experience acting and that you will more likely be a better on- camera actor than non-union actors. You will then be able to get better agents, invited to better auditions for better projects, have better working conditions, protections, and benefits provided by the union, and just have a better life as an actor in general. That's why everyone wants in. The only downside—if you want to call it that, I don't—is that you can no longer do non-union on-camera work, but hopefully you'll never sweat that as you book more lucrative and professional union projects moving forward. That's not to say that there aren't non-union projects out there that pay well and have professionally run productions; it's just that there is no guarantee of basic compensation or work conditions. The non-union world is the unregulated wild west of acting, and it's left to you and your team to determine which projects are professional and worthwhile and which are not.

I should also mention that even if you join the union, you can elect to give up basically all your union benefits to go "Financial Core" status, or better known as fi-core. That means you can do both union and non-union work because, some argue, a girl's gotta do what a girl's gotta do to put food on her family. It's a very controversial topic so I'll let you do your own research about it, but I will say that I personally would never go fi-core as I believe it cuts the legs out from under the union if you sell yourself for cheap on the side. It defeats the whole purpose of having a union. However, in order to make a living acting, people do what they feel they must in order to pay the bills. You can't eat your principles, as they say.

CHAPTER SEVENTEEN
What now?
The boring day-to-day life of an actor and how to kill time between jobs.

There you go. That's how the process works from beginning to end. Now that you're familiar with the life cycle of a booking, it's time to fill in the blanks as to what to do in between the jobs you book.

I. Training

Duh. If you were paying attention above, then you already know you should be training regularly in an improv class, an ongoing scene study, and hopefully an on-camera class as well. Training is one of five pillars that should support the day in and day out life of the professional working actor.

II. Submitting yourself for work

If you don't remember, let me remind you that you can submit yourself for castings on castingnetworks.com and castingfrontier.com. Do that religiously throughout the day, making sure you've signed up for email or text alerts when a role you're right for has been released. Especially until you have professional representation, this is the main way you will generate commercial opportunities for yourself. For theatrical work, take a look at actorsaccess.com and nowcasting.com.

III. Getting and working with your representation

If you don't have an agent, you should be doing all the things I listed in chapter seven. If you do have representation, you should be in regular communication with them as to what you can be doing to assist their efforts to market you and supporting that in every way you can.

IV. Casting workshops and showcases

Also, as I said in chapter seven about agent showcases, we are lucky to have direct access to casting directors, associates, and assistants through workshops and showcases. Participate whenever and as often as you can to get seen by casting professionals and be on their mind. Note that these workshops are technically for educational purposes only and are not an audition, but they are the best direct way to build a relationship with those casting offices and for them to become familiar with your work. Showcases and workshops with commercial CD's are less frequent for reasons I point out in the next chapter.

V. Create your own work

The equipment and software to create your own projects are essentially available to every actor. With just a little research, you can start to write, shoot, edit and publish shorts, web series, specs, sample scenes, whatever. Just create and do what makes you happy and shows off the parts of your talent that you're proud of. Here is the chance for you to play the roles you want to play, market yourself the way you want to be marketed, and grow as a talent and storyteller. If something hits and goes viral or gets someone's attention, it could be a career-maker. Just accept that the first few things you do are going to suck, but keep at it until they're merely just bad, and a few years later you'll be making things some people in other less developed counties might call passable when there's nothing better to watch on satellite cable.

In addition to the above, remember that you are a product that you are trying to hock all over this biz. Make sure you have the tools to market yourself. Put together a simple website with your photo and resume, bio, and your agent's contact information. Put together a one-minute reel and upload it to a video-sharing site like YouTube so you can be found and quickly share it with anyone interested.

DON'T BE AN L.A. FLAKE
I can't stress what I'm about to say enough, and I don't want to overload you with a whole paragraph in all caps, so I'm just going to have to ask you to take this section to heart as much, or more, than anything I've shared with you so far. I have found nothing to be truer in this business than the following: The more you give, the more you receive. No one builds an empire alone. Be the one who says yes, who shows up, attends their friends' shitty plays and improv shows, who holds the boom microphone for a stupid web short film shoot, who helps your friends rehearse before an audition, and who drives across town to support your friends and make new ones. As actors, we are each other's

greatest resource. Your chances of success exponentially increase if you build a strong network of other actors to rehearse with, put you on tape, learn with, produce with, perform with, and who will talk you off the ledge in your moments of weakness. We need each other to show up. We need each other to care and go the extra mile. If you commit yourself to giving as much of yourself as you can, without, of course, taking on too much or sacrificing your own progress, I can promise you'll have a more successful, rewarding, and joyful journey.

CHAPTER EIGHTEEN
Peon Love: How to get called in to more commercial casting offices.
(SPOILER: If you want to be interesting, be interested and don't be a dickhead.)

Because casting directors are constantly deluged by submissions from agents and managers and because commercial CD's have to call in a medium to high volume of talent for each role, they have the room in their audition schedules to try out some new faces on a daily basis and thus don't have to go see plays and showcases like theatrical CD's do in order to discover new talent. You won't see most of the busiest commercial CD's doing that stuff, which makes them harder to reach and connect with when you're trying to become one of the 50 people they'll call in for a role in your category out of the 2,000 submissions they're getting every time. Therefore, I teach one secret tip that is guaranteed to get their attention and make sure everyone in that office knows who you are and has an incentive to bring you in at least once to meet you and give you a chance.

What? You want me to just TELL you my secret tip? If I told you, it wouldn't be a secret, now would it? Think! I reserve this totally simple and effective tip for my actual, real life students. If you want this holy grail of all tips, you'll have to sign up for one of my commercial workshops or ongoing, on-camera acting classes. Sorry. I gave you the rest of this information for next to nothing, didn't I? Don't be so ungrateful. Look in the mirror and take a good look at the monster you've become. What happened to the down-to-earth person I once knew? You're so LA now!

I will, however, tell you my *other* powerful tip, which I briefly mentioned earlier on, which is to get to know your session directors, lobby assistants, casting assistants, and camera operators. We work all over town and will help you if we can and if we know and like you. And we will only know and like you if you made that happen, or if you are super awesome and talented and we made the effort to get to know you. Or it could just happen over time as we continue to see you at the offices when you do get auditions, but that leaves a lot up to chance and could take years, if ever, to develop. Take the bull by the horns. What, you think you're going to live forever?

Also, don't forget about the casting *associates*. They may not be the casting director, but they're essentially the right hand of the King/Queen, and some are even the power behind the throne, and they don't get as much love. If you want to charm an office, find out who the associate is, include them in your thoughts, prayers, and networking, and do the secret thing I'm refusing to tell you in this book.

WRAP IT UP, B
In the end, training to be the best actor you can be, creating your own work, getting in front of casting directors whenever possible through workshops and showcases, submitting yourself for work on and offline, getting great representation and working with them to

expand your opportunities for mutual success, being knowledgeable about the business and casting process, giving as much as you can of yourself to other actors, and being awesome to, and interested in, the people that make it all happen day-in and day-out is the best way to maximize your chances of success, not only as a commercial actor but as a professional actor, period.

Thank you for taking the time to read this book. I look forward to seeing you at your next audition, hopefully as an actor auditioning alongside you, but it's also possible that I will be running that session instead. Telling me you read this drivel will fill me with pride and earn you 50 brownie points towards our friendly professional relationship moving forward, so BONUS!

I hope that this information has been a helpful starting point in knowing what to do. Almost all of us move here from somewhere else with no good information as to how things actually work, and it can be so haphazard where you end up training and how you end up finding out the right information. It's my hope that this insider look into the world of commercial acting and casting helps you sidestep the mistakes I and others naturally made when we started out. A better-informed and trained acting community will only make my life easier in the casting studio. In fact, this material is actually all a selfish effort for my own benefit. But hey, if good is achieved with it also, well then that's extra karma for me.

On that note, let's say you actually enjoyed this book and found it very helpful and wanted to show me some appreciation for it. If you got your hands on this for free somehow, you could, theoretically, PayPal me a few bucks to shaan@shaansharma.com. What I would most appreciate, however, is if you shared this information with a few other actor friends so that they can be better informed, more successful, and know that I'm around as a resource.

Speaking of that, if you've somehow been bamboozled into thinking I know what I'm talking about and want MORE, then look me up on the interwebs, and you'll find plenty of opportunities to be personally trained by one of the luckiest and happiest people in the world. A guy that gets to pass the time between his own acting jobs working for the best companies, best CD's, best directors and production companies, and best fellow casting professionals in the world, helping other amazingly talented and skilled actors book work themselves. It's truly an honor to do what I do every day, and I look forward to each session where I can help create the kind of audition experience that I would want to audition in myself. If you ever catch me failing in that regard, know that something truly extraordinary was able to overwhelm my usual stalwart consistency and composure. It's not personal. Just don't try to shake my fucking hand.

Shaan Sharma

MY STORY: HOW DID I GET INTO CASTING?

Well, I started acting in Minnesota. I did that for 10 years until I finally resolved to move to LA. When I got here in 2007, it turns out that I shared a mutual friend with Joe Blake of Joe Blake Casting at Ocean Park Casting in Santa Monica. Joe is one of the busier commercial CD's in town. He met with me at our mutual friend's request and offered me a job running sessions. Within a couple weeks, I was doing it full-time. Once you get a good reputation working for a well-established CD, it gives other CD's confidence in hiring you as well. Within a year, I had branched out to working with a dozen top commercial CD's all over town at different facilities. It just kept growing from there.

As of this point, I've worked with (let's see if I can remember them all):

Joe Blake
Cathi Carlton
Michael Sanford
Ross Lacy
Brigid McBride
RMB Casting
Emma Nelson
Dan Cowan
Ava Shevitt
Petite Casting
Charisse Glenn
All Rhoades Casting
ASG
Liz Paulson
Jane Doe
Pop Casting
Skirts
Laurie Records
Beauregard Casting

Gabrielle Schary
Beth Holmes
Tolley Casparis
Lisa Fields
John McCarthy
Lisa Pantone
Digital Dogs
Tiffany Persons
Danielle Eskinazi
Melissa Feliciano
Spot Casting
Bokcreative
Sobo Casting
Pam Starks
Davis-Baddeley
Paul Weber
Amey Rene
Sonnenberg Casting

And those are just the ones I can remember. I'm missing a few. I know it. Sorry. I'm seven years in, man. It's all a blur.

ACKNOWLEDGMENTS
Special thanks to Michael Sanford, Cori Greenhouse, John Ruby, Charles Carpenter, Jessica Mullen, Tristin Rupp, Kelly Frye, Elisha Sum, Kevin Callahan, Troy

O'Brien, Stacey Atkinson and Erin Willard for their feedback, help and suggestions.

Thank you to my students for being the inspiration for this book.

BONUS CHAPTER NINETEEN
Mommy needs new Manolo Blahniks: How to pimp out your attention-starved child to make and hide enough money to divorce your cheating husband while accumulating legitimate bragging rights to shut up all those other bitches at your child's school who only THINK their kids are special while you have actual PROOF that yours is better because she booked a national network TV Jello commercial.

First off, I want to applaud you. My parents never considered how they could help me get a jump start on my acting or music career when I was a child, even though I showed early signs of intense interest in performing on-camera and playing music. Your child is extremely lucky to have at least one parent who cares about his or her interest in the arts and is willing to do what it takes to help him or her succeed.

Even if you or your child isn't interested in making a career out of acting as an adult, booking just ONE commercial could pay for their entire private school or college education, so it's not surprising that so many parents look into commercial acting for their kids. So here are some tips to help save you some money and help your child be more successful at it.

My mom did daycare in our home for twenty years. I grew up with ten kids in the house every day from 7am to 6pm between the ages of newborns to thirteen years. I did childcare myself after high school for two years as a Manny (male nanny). I adore kids. Working with them in castings is one of my specialties. What all that experience has taught me is that the best thing you can do to develop your child's ability to act and audition is to just be a great parent. Be fun, loving, patient, and supportive, and discipline firmly when necessary. I personally believe that the best thing you can do to help your young child thrive in acting (as well as in life) is maintain a healthy system of discipline, one that teaches them to have respect for others, especially adults, while not stifling their natural self-confidence and excitement.

Your young kids (under 6) don't need acting-specific training to book commercials. What we look for in children that young is that they are fun, talkative, good listeners, well-behaved, can follow specific directions, confident, and playful with us and other actors. We just need those kids to be kids. They just need to be themselves. Unlike many adults who learn to repress their natural love of others and emotions, fear judgment and care so much about looking "cool," kids are open, free, and vibrant. They say awesome, silly things. They just want to have fun and love others. Please reinforce these qualities in your children. Don't squash them. As long as they can focus when asked, don't drill them like sergeants in the military.

The best way to ensure your child will not book anything is to stress out about it yourself or stress them out about it. Just make acting a fun thing you do in addition to all the other wonderful activities you do together. If you put pressure on kids, they clam up or shut down. Their little brains start to short-circuit.

You can see it happen. It's heart-breaking. Keep it fun and light or don't put your family through it.

The kids that don't book are the ones that are too shy or quiet, who can't settle down and focus, are mean or disrespectful, are spoiled little brats, or OBVIOUSLY DON'T WANT TO BE THERE. If it's clear that your child doesn't like acting or auditioning, don't make him or her. Have another child and pray they will enjoy it.

All children are different and develop at different rates. Some 5-year-olds can handle dialogue while others can barely state their name. Once you get into the 6-8 range, we can expect most of them to be able to follow directions pretty well. So it's about that point where I'd advise getting them into plays or kid's acting classes or camps. I can't personally recommend any specific classes yet because there aren't that many and I don't know much about them. Please send me your feedback about any you try.

HEADSHOTS

The above chapter on headshots doesn't really apply as much to kids. You just need a good, even inexpensive but still nice, shots of their faces. Their normal faces, not gussied up like Honey Boo Boo. For roles, minors tend to get broken into age groups like newborns (0–3 months), infants (3–24 months), toddlers (2–4ish), young kids 5–8, kids 9–12, young teens 13–15, and older teenagers 16–18. I would advise updating their headshots when they are clearly in the next age tier of kids roles. Make sure they're smiling in the shots. We need to see the condition of their teeth and if they have braces. It's not a deal-breaker if they don't have perfect teeth, we just don't want to be surprised.

BE AN ASSET TO YOUR CHILD, NOT A LIABILITY

We've all heard of "stage parents." I guess it's the acting equivalent of parents of kids in sports who get a little too carried away on the sidelines. I guess the best advice I can give you is to just be reasonable, educated and cool. Study the SAG-AFTRA rules and advice for parents. Be prepared for and punctual to your child's auditions. Be patient, generous, and good-natured at castings and on set. Stay out of the way while also keeping a watchful, protective eye on your child. A good parent of a child actor should be like a great waiter at a restaurant: being attentive while not being seen or heard more than necessary. Focus on being helpful but not overbearing and supportive, not competitive. Concerns about you being a pain in the clients' ass will be reason enough to not book your child.

GETTING THEM REPRESENTED AND WORK

Submit them online for jobs and do mass mailings to agents until they are old enough to do workshops and showcases.

YOUR BROOD

Just because one of your kids got an audition, doesn't mean you can bring all your other kids and expect them to be able to audition too. Whoever got the audition is the only person we want to see unless another child is an exact fit for a role we're casting and you cleared it with us ahead of time.

PARTING GENERAL TIPS

You might want to carry some treats with you to give to all the actors whose knees you accidentally nail with your Jeep Grand Cherokee 4x4 Stroller.

As much as I am theoretically totally against it, for your sanity and those around you in lobbies at auditions, get your children, with their tiny, poor, developing, impressionable minds, hopelessly addicted to mobile devices so they'll be quiet and sit still.

With children, especially under six years old, we get what we get. You can't expect young children to be able to perform or audition on cue. Many times, after you've moved mountains to get your child to an audition, they simply won't want to do it and if they don't feel like doing it, we can't make them, and neither should you, for the sake of your soul, if nothing else.

If you're a single parent, dress to impress for every one of your child's auditions. You know the other parents there get down and you know that some of them had to turn sex into work instead of pleasure to conceive, so they are dying to PAR-TAY.

If you're the one with an audition and you have kids, feel free to bring them with you. As long as they know to keep quiet and not interrupt the audition, they can come right into the studio with you and can sit at our desk or on our client couches or chairs. If you know they can't *not* interrupt or disturb the session, hire a sitter. You could leave them in the lobby while you audition, and I've never heard of children disappearing from there, but, as a matter of principle, you should avoid it at all costs. It will put them in a nearly-negligible amount of danger and distract you. Yes, chances are there will be friendly actors or lobby assistants there who COULD and will keep an eye on them for you, but it's not their job to, it's not fair to expect them to, nor is it appropriate for you to distract them from focusing on their preparation for their own auditions.

tl;dr: if your kids can't behave, don't bring them.

**OKAY.
THIS IS THE END OF THE BOOK, NOW.
SEE YOU LATER. BYE.**

SAMPLE RESUME

Bob Lobla
SAG-AFTRA (if non-union, then nothing)

Height: 9'   Weight: 585   Eyes: Black   Hair: I wish

TV:

The Name of the Show	Role Type	Network/Director
Example Show	Co-Star	BBTV/Dir: Dick Likey
Cop Drama 15	Guest Star	RAT/Dir: Boobface McGee
Hot Whiney Twentysomethings	Series Regular	MUD/Dir: Creepy Huggerson

Film:

The Name of the Film	Role Type	Studio/Director
Human Millipede	Lead	Werner Bros./Dir: Ham Anchees
Botany for Liberals	Supporting	Hippie Films/Dir: Sunshine Rainbow

Theater:

The Name of the Play	Role Name	Theater Name/Location
Jofess and the Unicolor Swimsuit	Rango	Tiny Theater/Nowhere, UT
The Worst Big Convent in MN	Rupert	Red Box Theater/Hatsville, MI
Dudes and Babes	Meanly-Meanly	UH Theater/Big Island, HI
Oboist on the Ceiling	Pantsy	Soap Theater/Cox Penitentiary, NY

Commercial: Conflicts upon request.

Training:

Training Type	Studio Name	Teacher Name if other than Studio
Comedy Intensive	Schmesly John & Co.	Schmesly John
Clinic/Ongoing	Schmesly John & Co.	Fanny Overhang
Improv - ongoing	ColdStick Improv	Jenny Fromtheblock
Improv	Downright Foreigner Person	Chief Running Mouth
Scene Study	Dr. Glasses LaTweed	

Dialects: East Anglian
Skills: Singing (Tenor), Acoustic and Bass Guitar, Piano, Firearms, Wedding DJ

Theatrical:	Commercial:	Manager: Jan Tan
The Award Agency	AOA Talent Agency	Idiot Talent Collective
(310) 123-4567	(323) 987-6543	(911) 911-9119
www.gimmeawards.com	www.aoatalent.com	www.idiotsrus.com

SOCIAL MEDIA LINKS

 facebook.com/shaansharmaactingstudio

 @shaansharma

www.shaansharma.com

shaan@shaansharma.com

www.ingramcontent.com/pod-product-compliance
Lightning Source LLC
Chambersburg PA
CBHW060952230426
43665CB00015B/2173